The Power of a
DREAM

The Power of a
DREAM

Cindi Jasa

Beatrice Machamire-Ogomo

THE POWER OF A DREAM

©2017 Cynthia Jasa. All Rights Reserved.
Cj.yolt@gmail.com

For publishing inquiries, contact:
YOLT Publishing
c/o CMI
13518 L Street
Omaha, NE 68137

ISBN: 978-0-9982931-1-0

Publishing and production services by Concierge Marketing Inc.

Library of Congress and Cataloging-in-Publication
data on file with the publisher

Printed in the USA
10 9 8 7 6 5 4 3

Contents

We would like to dedicate this book to the many people in Africa who helped make our visit so amazing! Thanks for welcoming us into your lives!

We also want to thank so many of our family and friends who contributed towards our trip either through prayers, shoe donations or financial support. None of this would have happened without you. To say we are grateful wouldn't begin to express how we feel about you!

Thank you to our husbands and children (and grandchildren) who encouraged and supported us both in the preparation and during our trip. Thanks for believing in us!

We also want to thank everyone who has helped us in the process of this book, and for each one who was mentioned in the contents. What would we do without you? From the editing, proof-reading, designing the cover, the logo, and other suggestions given, you were the sounding board and the inspiration we needed to complete this book well. It takes a village!

Part of this writing is about my story. The other part is about Beatrice and her story. I hope you get a glimpse of how God can use two very different people from two very different cultures to join forces and partner together in His work.

This book will be taking some detours so please enjoy the journey with us. We have so much in our hearts that we want to share and it's hard to even know where to begin. With that in mind, let's get started and see just what can happen when God gives two people a dream and they choose to pursue it!

About the Authors

Cindi Jasa was born in Omaha, Nebraska and still resides there with her husband, Doug. They have two sons, two daughters-in-law and nine grandchildren.

Beatrice Machamire-Ogomo was born and raised in Zimbabwe, Africa. She now lives in Frisco, Texas with her husband, John, and their three boys.

Cindi & Beatrice

Growing Up - My Beginning

Cindi

I grew up as the youngest in a family of six children. We were very close in age (my oldest sister is just six years older than I am and she was born about a month before my parents' first anniversary!). We were a middle class family. We had all that we needed and I never remember a time that I lacked anything. We didn't have an abundance of things but we definitely had enough. We took a family vacation every year and enjoyed life.

My dad owned an appliance store not far from our house and my mom worked with him. Both of my parents worked very hard to provide for us. We actually had a cleaning lady whose name was Beatrice.

I had a normal childhood (at least in my eyes). I was a good kid but definitely not the favorite (my siblings didn't like it when I told on them). I was known as the "goody-goody" of the family because I liked to play by the rules. I got above average grades in school and for the most part, did what I was told. I got married young and started my new life as a wife.

My mom died at the age of 49 of a malignant brain tumor. She and I had not yet gotten to the point of becoming 'adult friends'. My oldest son (and only one at the time) was 9 months old when she died. It's hard for me that my boys and their families never knew my mom and the thoughtful person she was. (I now have two boys with very big hearts, two wonderful daughters-in-love, and nine amazing grandchildren.)

I remember my mother's generosity, especially around the holidays. She would invite people who had nowhere else to go. There were so many of us that a few more didn't make much of a difference. She and I loved Jesus and we both had a love for music. I remember her taking me to a few concerts at different churches when I was younger.

As hard as it was for me to lose my mother at age 23, I knew she was in heaven and that I would see her again one day. I stayed strong and moved forward with my life and my faith, still feeling the void left by her absence.

On the other hand, my dad grew up in some hard circumstances. He never talked much about his family. One of his brothers drowned at a young age and another one was given to his mother's sister who was unable to conceive children of her own (this was not that uncommon back then). Even though he was very good with people and conversations (small talk), he didn't know how to have a personal relationship with us. My siblings and I all knew that he loved us. He just didn't know how to show it. And even though my father lived a long life, not many of his grandchildren (and he had many!) had much of a relationship with him either.

I am a much different person now than I was back then. I have loved Jesus for as long as I can remember, but my actions didn't always show it. I thought I was following God, but I didn't know that He wanted to give me direction in EVERY area of my life. I thought I was supposed to make my decisions and then God would 'bless' them.

That might sound silly to those of you who know better, but for many of us, that's how it was (or still is). Over the years I have made some major choices that weren't always the best, but God either has or is turning them into good because He promises to do that in Romans 8:28 (*"And we know that all that happens to us is working for our good if we love God and are fitting into His plans."*). He promises to do that because I love Him.

After I got married, I was always the one in charge of the finances in our home. I did a pretty good job with what we made (which wasn't very much in the beginning), but I lived in fear that we might not have enough. I was not a very generous person. In fact, I was pretty tight with our money. I remember one time my husband went to lunch with a missionary couple who were raising support. He told them we would help them but I never sent any money. I still regret that to this day.

My Family

Doug and Cindi

Nick, Ethan, Caleb, Emily, Eliza, Caryn, Xander, Evlyn, Bri

Carly, Mike, Brynn, and Zeke

My Family

Beatrice

In the small African village of Tandi, two brothers, Hedrick (my biological father) and Newton Machamire met two sisters, Shine (my biological mom) and Grace. Back in their day, proposals were usually based on a family's reputation and the chastity of their daughters. As destiny would have it, Hedrick and Newton decided they were going to marry Shine and Grace. After a short courtship, the two couples got married and started their families.

Before my parents met they both had other children from their previous marriages. Together they only had me as a child. From what I am told, my parents loved each other dearly and dreamt of a wonderful future together where they would raise all their children in the best possible way they could.

Unfortunately, it was never meant to be. In December of 1985 when I was 10 months old, my father was involved in a fatal car accident. He had been traveling from Headlands to Harare. His death was very sudden and left my mother a single parent with no one to support her and her three children. Being a widow in Africa is not easy simply because a woman's worth, especially back in the day, was measured by her marital status and bliss – or lack of. The men took pride in providing for their families to which they would get credit and accolades.

I can't even imagine how my mother was doomed to struggle as a single mother with her three children to take care of. And struggle she did for a period of two years where she managed to single handedly take care of us. She was a very hardworking woman. She used to raise chickens to sell. She would also knit and sew.

Her saving grace came in the form of her sister Grace who had married Newton (my father's brother). They were staying in a small town called Chinhoyi, which thrived on commercial farming. Their offer to my mother was to take care of one child out of her three. It was easier (for them) to choose me considering they were my aunt and uncle. This meant that I could live a better life, go to a better school and be raised together with my cousins. But it also meant that life for my two siblings whom I would be leaving behind would not be as rosy.

So at the tender age of 3 1/2 years old, I was sent to Chinhoyi to begin my new life with my extended family. I learned how to call my aunt and uncle "mom" and "dad", which is very common in my culture, the same way we refer to cousins as siblings. In this new family of mine, no one could tell that I wasn't their biological child. My biological mother would often visit. I wonder how she must have felt as my new "siblings" and I called her aunty!

My parents did their best to raise us. They would discipline us whenever disciplinary action was needed, even though the others were spanked more than I was. If I remember correctly I was only spanked twice, whereas my brother and sister got a lot more spankings dished out to them. My sister Victoria would often pay for my sins. She knew that I wasn't very used to being spanked so whenever I did something wrong or when she made me do something wrong, she would take the spanking on my behalf. What more could I ask for? I was considered the saint of the house and my mother would often praise me and brag about me to her friends. With a strong belief in *Spare the rod, spoil the child'*, we all certainly turned out to be great achievers who today have made our parents very proud and honorable in their community.

As I adjusted, settled and grew within my family, I never lacked anything. From school, clothes, and books - you name it – it was all provided for with love. That was true for all of us.

Tithing

Cindi

Over the years, God began to change my heart. I don't remember exactly when I realized the need for tithing. If this is a concept that's new to you, it simply means that you give the first 10% of your income back to God. The truth is, it all belongs to Him anyway, and He distributes the wealth as He chooses. All He asks is that we give back His portion (the tithe). He allows us to keep the rest (the 90%).

The ultimate plan is that we use the remainder wisely, with God's direction. What many people don't understand is that when they keep it all for their own use, they end up further behind, not farther ahead. The tithe will disappear and they will be in a worse state than if they had been obedient. It may be swallowed up by unexpected bills such as a higher amount owed on a tax return, doctor bills, car repairs or numerous other expenses. God can actually do more with 90% of our income than we can with 100%. It's one of those mysteries that we can't seem to figure out. If we try to do the math, it won't work out on paper.

I have heard so many stories about how God came through in unexpected ways when people were obedient with the tithe. The only way to explain many of these scenarios is to realize that God showed up and did a miracle. No other explanation would make any sense.

I remember at one point in our lives (not all that long ago) when I struggled with the tithe. The battle wasn't about whether or not to give it, but when. We owned our own business so the employees, bills and business expenses were my first concern.

I call this the time when I 'collected pay checks'. We got paid every two weeks. I would usually get to the third paycheck before I could cash one. I always had a stash of uncashed paychecks in my possession. My question was, "Do I tithe before or after I actually cash the check?" Honestly, I don't remember what my final decision was on that.

God has brought us a long way since that time but I treasure that time of teaching and testing. Did you know that money is the only area in the Bible where God says to test Him?

Malachi 3:10 says, *"Bring all the tithes into the storehouse so that there will be food enough in My Temple; if you do, I will open up the windows of heaven for you and pour out a blessing so great you won't have room enough to take it in!* **Try it! Let Me prove it to you!"**

The blessings don't always come in monetary form, but God does promise to meet our needs (not our 'greeds'). Maybe too much money would lead many to think that they don't really need God because they have plenty and seem to get along just fine on their own. On the other hand, if they have to depend on Him to provide what is needed, that just might be what draws someone closer to God, where they can experience Him as their Provider.

Beatrice

My husband John doesn't have a problem with tithing at all. In fact he's the one who makes sure that we give our tithe any time we have income. He also makes sure that we tithe from our tax returns (I know many people have a different interpretation of tithing from tax returns).

The truth is, it remains a mystery how God looks at it, but I believe that He looks at the heart. I have heard so many sermons about tithing and not all of them appealed to me. I always felt that if the tithe was going to be used to bless the poor, orphans and widows, I might as well make the process easier for the church so I would do it myself. I would sometimes take part, or even all, of the tithe to help a relative in need.

Obviously, part of the reason was because after I paid all the bills and I only had the tithe left and then a need arose, I would turn back to the tithe. That is still a problem for me until now. When everything is okay I don't mind tithing at all. But when there are certain things that need attention, I struggle. And when I talk of attention I don't necessarily mean my personal needs. I tend to think that if someone is in need I could just take the tithe, help the said person and take the remainder to church! Logical isn't it? Yet God's ways and instructions defy all logic!

However, in my walk of faith I am learning a lot. I remember Cindi asking us one time if we tithed and I was honest enough to tell her that we do try and tithe but we had other commitments and other people to help and that it wasn't always easy to tithe. The truth is, tithing is definitely a choice that one has to make and it's not always the easy choice. It's a strong leap of faith, but I have to admit that I have noticed what God does in our lives when we obey Him. I'm not only talking of financial blessings but a profound abundance in all areas of life.

One of the times that God made His promise come true was when I was selected as a winner of the green card lottery. Over 10 million applicants registered for this lottery and only 50 thousand were selected. I 'happened' to be among the 50 thousand who were selected! I was ecstatic! It obviously might not seem like a huge thing to most people but part of the reason why I could not get employed in the US was because I didn't have a work permit or a green card. That meant if I was to go back to Zimbabwe and visit my family, I wouldn't have been able to come back to the US, even though my husband and kids were here. My husband and I had been applying for the green card every year for about 10 years and we had not been selected. So you can imagine our joy when we were finally selected - pure bliss!

Why am I saying this? I will share this story in short. About two years before I was selected for the green card lottery, there was a series at church about giving extravagantly and the pastor challenged the congregation to give towards purchasing a new building for a satellite campus. My husband and I were definitely not in a position to give much. In fact, I remember telling myself that this challenge was for those who had the financial means. But through my husband's obedience, God gave him an amount to contribute. He asked me if I had come up with a number and I sure had, but it was nowhere close to what he had come up with. I decided not to argue about it because we were to pledge an amount and then pay it over two years. After making the calculations, it still didn't add up.

I was wondering what John must have been thinking. Surely it didn't make any sense at all but that's what happens with things of God's Kingdom. I was thinking that I had so many relatives that I could have helped with all that money. Nothing seems to make sense when we try to look at it with our natural eyes, but it surely does make sense when God is in charge. I reluctantly agreed to the amount and my husband assured me that we could do it.

This also happened to be the time when we weren't so sure about our immigration status. We either had to stay in the US illegally or go back to Kenya or to Zimbabwe. Since we were from different countries we didn't know where exactly to go. The US seemed to be pretty neutral ground for both of us, considering that we had already raised our children and started our family over here. However we thought we would leave it all to Christ.

My point is that we both decided to obey God by giving what we didn't have. I believe God answered our prayers because of our leap of faith. We had been applying for the green card for about nine years and each year would come and pass and we would reapply but we were never selected. Finally God showed up on our doorstep in 2014 and we were able to go back to our home countries and visit our families. I know that the purpose of giving shouldn't be so that you get something back, but when it's done out of faith and obedience, God will surely reward in many different ways.

Cindi - Continued

I just want to add that if tithing was easy and made perfect sense, it would take no faith to do so. God loves to reward us for trusting Him to do all that He has promised, but His rewards come in response to our obedience. Money is one of the things Jesus talked about the most because our hearts seem to follow our finances. What we value most becomes what we serve.

Most people say that if they had more money, they would be happy to tithe. But did you know that people with more money actually have a harder time tithing than those who have little? That's because if you make a lot of money, 10% can seem like a huge amount. But if you have been giving faithfully from the beginning when you didn't have so much, then it's just becomes the natural thing to do. You have already experienced God's blessings and learned to trust Him with little. That usually means that He can also trust you with much.

It's good to start right where you are in life. I think it's especially good if you are taught to tithe as a child so it becomes a natural part of your life and of your routine. Then when you are older, tithing is already a part of what you do.

I have tested God over and over and He has been faithful to His Word. But since this book isn't about tithing (although it will be weaved throughout the pages), I need to continue with my story. I'd like to share some highlights from my journey along the way, leading up to the greatest adventure I've been called to participate in so far.

Christmas Blessings

Christmas Parties - Cindi

One of my highlights for the past 15 years is a Christmas party I have for women every year (I actually got the idea from a friend). It started small and continued to grow over the years. The best part of it was that every year was a new idea from God. I always said that if it got down to only what I wanted to do or could dream up, I would stop hosting them, because God is so creative and I love how He blesses the women when they come!

The hardest part for me was waiting for God to show me His plan for that year. Sometimes it would come right away (like the day after the last party) and other times I felt like it wasn't ever going to come.

Every year had a 'theme'. I remember the year I called "The Bride of Christ". It was about how loved we are and that Jesus wants us to be His bride. I even found my wedding dress to display. There is always a song involved because I relate best through music.

That particular year I was assisting a young lady with her wedding. She wanted poinsettias for her flowers. I told her I would purchase them but I would like to have them for my party after the wedding. We planned the dates accordingly and I went to Sam's Club to order the flowers. We were all set to go – or so I thought.

I went to pick the flowers up the day of the wedding and they didn't have them there! I had two choices – to panic and get angry or trust God to show up. Fortunately, I choose the latter response. And guess what? He showed up in a BIG way.

The store manager began to call their other stores and sent people out to gather the plants. I waited until the plants arrived and watched the employees as they cut, watered and took extra care with each one. When they were almost done, I went over to pay for them (it was about $200 worth of poinsettias) and the manager said he was giving them to me for free! Talk about a God story!!

But I had another moment after that when I was driving down the street and I was telling the Lord, "These plants aren't going to be special because I didn't have to pay for them." I will never forget His answer to me. He spoke to my heart and said "Tell them they are from ME!" I got tears in my eyes. What would you rather receive, a gift from the hostess or from God? He wanted to bless "His bride".

I had poinsettias (probably 50 of them) lining my whole living room and hallway! They were beautiful. They seemed to be everywhere and each lady got to take home as many as she wanted!! I was even told by a few of the women that they lasted longer than any other poinsettias they had ever received!

I think you can get a glimpse of why I love these parties so much! Take that one times 15 and you might understand why I look forward to them. The past two years we have even been blessed with valet parking by some of the men from my church! They have spoiled us and we love it!

Since I have more stories than I have pages, I will move on.

Blessing Bags

Cindi

Well, maybe I won't move on quite that fast. I have to tell you about the year God gave me the idea of the "Blessing Bags". At this point in my life, I love to give. It brings me more joy than anything I could ever do or buy for myself and I was trying to think of a way to pass that joy along to others.

I thought of giving out random sums of money for people to use in some creative way to bless another person. I was struggling to come up with an amount that would be just right. God and I were having a discussion about it and I felt like $5.00 was the amount He gave me. It wasn't a lot so it would be an amount that most people could manage to do on their own. I felt good about the decision and began making bags.

I challenged people with my 'Mission Impossible' theory. I wanted to see if they could help me out-give God. I knew it wasn't possible. I just wanted to prove it. After they decided what to do with the money, I asked them to send me an email and let me know what they did. That way I could share in the blessing (and maybe get some new ideas)!

I have to share one story that was told to me from a recent bag I gave out. A mother explained to her 4 year old son what the money was for and gave it to him to decide what to do with it. He put it away in his wallet. Christmas came and went and he still had the money.

One cold January day they were out driving around and saw a homeless lady on the street with a sign. The mom told him what it said and he knew immediately what to do. They drove through KFC and purchased her a hot meal. When they took it to her, she got tears in her eyes because people weren't stopping to help and she was hungry. Needless to say, that mom gave her son another $5 bill to use in the future!

I especially love teaching children how to be a blessing because they seem to 'get it' even better than adults. Sometimes I believe they are more sensitive to what God tells them to do than adults are. That may happen because children aren't as busy or as preoccupied as adults so they can hear God more clearly. I also think they are more likely to give without conditions attached.

I remember a lot of tears that first year as I read the stories of what many people had done to touch another life. It was one of my best Christmas' ever. The next year I put together a short booklet of many of their stories.

But the story didn't stop there. We have a friend who worked for Reader's Digest at the time. They always gave their employees a Christmas bonus but that particular year they decided to do something a little different. They gave each employee and their family members a small gift to pass on and be a blessing to someone else. Can you guess what that amount was? I think you probably can. It was $5.00!

Then I was blessed again. I had given one of the bags to each of our pastors. One Sunday when I came to church, someone said to me, "You're going to love what happens today". I remember one part of the service – the end. Our pastor did a 'reverse offering'. He told everyone to come up and take $5.00 (are you surprised by the amount?) out of the offering plate and use it to bless someone! He hadn't had time to read my letter. God had given him the same idea that He had given to me. I was blessed beyond belief!!

I have continued to do this every year since then on a smaller scale, but that year was definitely my favorite. And my theory proved true...it wasn't possible to out-give God. He has proved that over and over in my life and the joy I receive back is sometimes more than I can take in!

God Words

Cindi

Over the past several years I have had many 'God words' (things God has said to me through other people) spoken over me that were very encouraging but didn't always make a lot of sense. I'd like to share some of those with you to set the stage for what is happening in my life today.

Let me start with Hebrews 10:23. "Let's keep a firm grip on the promises that keep us going. He *always* keeps His Word." That verse and these words have encouraged me through the years.

Nov 16, 2005

"I will be a minister of the Gospel."

I believe this one started when my dad entered a nursing home after his stroke. One Easter he wanted to go to church with us and I told him he should go to the service there. He said there wasn't one. That took me by surprise.

But I was even more baffled when God said "YOU do it!" I remember asking, "WHO do it?" He assured me that I was the one He had chosen, even though others voiced their doubts about it. We overcame the obstacles we were faced with and ended up with a room of about 75 people (residents and family members) who came for the Easter service. I was even able to recruit a piano and a trumpet player.

We began holding services once a month there and I was so blessed by that. I believe my dad was blessed also. He would invite everyone he knew (and didn't know!). My family and friends would come along to help and I loved watching my grandchildren push wheelchairs down the hallway! That was an amazing time for me.

May 2006

"God has a hold of my hand and He's running.
My feet aren't even touching the ground!"

That one is happening right now, but more on that story later!

October 2006

"God wants me to be a leader, not a follower.
He has already given me all that I need. I just
have to believe it!"

I have always found it easier to be a follower because a leader has too much responsibility. I'm not fully there yet but I'm heading in the right direction!

August 14, 2012

"Don't put away my running shoes. Keep them
by my bedside because the day will come when
I find the joy of the Lord bubbling up in me."

"God has called me to have an integral part in
compassion ministry towards others."

This particular one excited and frightened me at the same time. I liked the part about the joy bubbling up in me and I have felt that many times since. It shows up when I really sense that I am right where God wants me to be. I have done some compassion things in the past, but I had no idea where God was going to take me with that one!

"How I was and how I'm going to be will be drastically different".

All I can say to that one is AMEN!

"Get my heart ready because I'm about to get into some exciting times in letting the Lord use me in powerful ways. My glory days are not behind, they're ahead!"

I am beginning to see this one... I believe I'm only seeing the tip of the iceberg right now but it is very exciting!

August 2014

"I have a grace for people of other cultures and for people who just don't get it. But I have the grace of Jesus to bring forth from the complex to the simple and to help people understand what He's all about and how much He loves

people. God will also be increasing the burden in my heart for the nations." (Isaiah 49: 6 "I will make you a light to the nations of the world, to bring my salvation to them.)."

I really didn't know at the time how this one applied to me. I'm pretty happy to be a city girl. I was very content to serve God from the comfort of my own home and in my home town. When I was doing services at the nursing home, my goal was to break down my message to a level that the people there could easily understand.

In 2015, God put it on my heart to write a book. I had wanted to do that for many years (maybe 20 or so?) but I knew this was the right time. I had a few ideas of what I wanted to write about, but God seemed to have a different plan. After revising it for the third time, it ended up being a simple story of God and His love for mankind. I titled it 'YOLT' (You Only Live Twice). I can't begin to describe how amazing it is that God would choose to partner with me to do this work with Him. It is very humbling.

So, are you getting the idea that God has plans for me? Many times God gives us a word that is for later. When most of these were spoken, I had no idea how they applied to me. I tried to 'fit them in' to my current life, but that didn't seem to work. As time went on and I went back to them, I was amazed at how my life was unfolding. It was happening just as He had spoken!

Beatrice

*These were words spoken over me many years ago. I have been encouraged every time I read them. God is not done with me yet. He is working on me in so many ways and I've seen some of it come to pass.

"You are like Esther - a woman of authority and dignity. It reminds me of how Queen Esther spoke before the King, asking for the lives of her people. I don't know exactly how God is going to use it but I believe you have a boldness and authority to speak up for His name. I feel like you have a zeal for that."

"The Lord calls you great in His kingdom, and you are faithful to the Lord and to your family. The Lord delights in you and He's inviting you to a place of deeper intimacy. In this season of life there have been ups and downs but He's working in you an eternal way to glory. He sees your heart and is pleased with you. If you look back it doesn't seem like you are getting very far. It feels like you are treading in the mud. You are running a race of perseverance and this race is tailored just for you. You should not look to the right or to the left or compare

yourself with others. You are doing a good job with what the Lord has set before you."

"I see you ministering to others in the years to come based on what you have learned. You are learning a lot and the way your heart is growing for the love of Jesus is invaluable. Your roots are going deeper in Him. I want to encourage you not to judge where you see yourself as compared to others because you are storing up treasures in heaven. You will also use what you have learned to encourage others."

A New
Friendship Begins

A New Friend - Cindi

In about 2010, God brought a very special lady into my life. I was given her name by my church as a family to bless at Christmas time. I tried many times to contact her and I was about to give up trying. I went to her apartment one last time and she was home.

Her name is Beatrice Machamire Ogomo and her husband is John. They had two small boys at the time named Daniel and Micah. I explained to her why I was there and she reluctantly gave me a small wish list. What impressed me most was the list she didn't give me. She had a list of things on her refrigerator that she would buy for herself when she had the money to do so – like a hand held can opener.

I thought that I was finished with what God had asked me to do and that after Christmas, my life would just continue as before (city girl – home town – you get the picture!). But He was working in me through Beatrice and I didn't even realize it at the time.

I don't recall all the details but I knew they could use some extra money and I also knew she wouldn't just continue to take money from me without some way to earn it. Beatrice said she was starting a cleaning business so I hired her to clean for me. Her charges were way below the current rate so I enjoyed blessing her with more than she asked for. And every time (even years later) she would thank me for the blessing. I never felt she expected more or took it for granted.

I had no idea how Beatrice was spending the money I gave her but I knew it was helping their situation. And I felt very confident that whatever I gave her was being put to good use.

As the years went on, we would have conversations while she was in my home. I wish I could say I always listened closely but that wasn't the case. She was a little hard for me to understand so it didn't register when she told me where she was from (Zimbabwe, Africa). I didn't really think it mattered anyway (I think we've established that I'm a city girl.). I guess

I was usually a little too busy to take time to listen closely. I wish I had those times back now!

I have had several God-ordained friendships over the years but my relationship with Bea was completely different. God had a special purpose in bringing us together as friends.

From the first time I met Bea, I saw her humble spirit and her heart for others. She was not only humble but trustworthy, and I could tell that she used wisely the things and the finances that God had given to her. She opened my eyes to a whole new world (literally) and a way of living that I had never experienced.

Sometimes her stories make me laugh and other times they bring tears to my eyes. This has been such a new and exciting adventure and I look forward to what else God has in store for us as our friendship continues to grow. Only God would think to put two totally different people together to change a little piece of the world! I am forever grateful that He put Beatrice in my life!

How I met Cindi - Beatrice

It was just before Christmas in 2010 when Cindi came knocking on my apartment door. I looked through the peep hole and noticed a silver haired woman standing on the other side. I thought she must have the wrong apartment. I went on to open the door and greeted her. She then asked if I was Beatrice and I told her yes, still trying to figure out what this woman would want with me. She told me that she attended Lifegate Church and that she had gotten my name from someone there and wanted to bless my family for Christmas. I thought to myself, "Why in the world would anyone want to bless strangers for Christmas? Didn't she have anything better to do with her money?" I told her it was so kind of her to do that and I didn't really know what to say at the moment.

She went on to ask me for my family's Christmas wish list. Fortunate enough I had a list of items that were on my wish list. It wasn't necessarily for Christmas, so I thought maybe I would give that to her after she insisted on me giving her the list. She then told me that she had come to my apartment several times and had missed me. This day that I finally was home and opened the door would have been her last attempt. So I gave her the list and she left, with a promise to return.

And return she did, a day or two later. I was a bit unprepared for this return visit. She came back with bags of wrapped Christmas gifts for my two children Daniel and Micah. I was in awe and at the same time, very grateful, that God had chosen our family that Christmas to be recipients of this woman's generosity and amazing show of love. The truth of the matter is that John and I were not even going to buy Christmas gifts for each other that Christmas due to financial constraints. If I recall correctly, we only had about two gifts under the Christmas tree for our two boys.

This same year also happened to be the year that my younger sister back in Zimbabwe had just been accepted into college. She had no one to pay for her college tuition and automatically I had to step in. I was also at this time paying tuition for my other younger sister who was in boarding school. The fact that I wasn't working and had two young boys at home meant that getting a full time job would have been more stressful because of all the daycare costs in the US! I decided I needed a part time solution. I knew I had to make a sacrifice for my sisters to go to school so I thought of doing something that could bring cash immediately.

A few weeks before Cindi came knocking at my door I had started a cleaning business. I only had two clients when I met Cindi, who became my third and eventually my only and consistent client. I struggled with this business idea because my ego was telling me that I had a college degree and was cut out to do something better than cleaning, like working for one of the large accounting and finance companies in Nebraska. I struggled with this for a while until I had to let go of my pride and do what had to be done.

I had felt so bad receiving all those gifts from Cindi without having "earned" them. It was just too much for us to receive these gifts from someone we didn't even know. In my effort to thank her, I told her about my cleaning business and that if she needed anyone to clean her house, I would be her person. I thought she was going to take time to respond but right there and then she said that she actually did need help cleaning her house. Her spontaneous response almost made it seem as if it was planned. I could not wait to share the good news with my husband. It was going to be a merry Christmas after all! She had bought everything that was on my wish list plus more.

We exchanged numbers and we agreed that she was to let me know when I could start cleaning her house. I impatiently waited for that phone call as I was desperately in need of more clients and extra cash for my younger sister's tuition. If I remember well, I started cleaning Cindi and Doug's (her husband) house about a week afterwards. That was just before Christmas and she needed me to come clean again after Christmas. She asked me how much I charged per hour, but she thought that I charged too little so she paid me way more than my hourly rate. God really provided in such a way I never thought He would. He always made a way when there seemed to be no way.

I never told Cindi why I was cleaning but somehow she seemed to know that I was in need. She kept asking me to come clean even when her house was squeaky clean. She would even ask me to go clean at her two son's houses and pay me handsomely. I had no idea at that time that God had something great ahead for us. All I was doing was making sure that I did my job and she made sure that she paid me well.

I remember her asking me if my other clients tipped me well and I told her that they only paid me what I charged them (or sometimes they came up with reasons to pay me less than I charged them). She told me that wasn't good. After a while I even dropped the other two clients. Cindi became my only client. She helped us a lot and I kept wondering why on earth she would do that. I was always very grateful.

I quickly learned how Cindi lived her life by being around her. I kept telling myself that I would want to be like her one day. Cindi is such a giver and as I cleaned, I would notice different things around her home which clearly showed me how to live life to the fullest. There was such peace in her home. She trusted me so much that she gave me her garage code and I would even clean when she wasn't home. I kept thanking God for bringing someone into my life that would trust me like that.

Cindi's smile is just priceless - she couldn't even hide it. Her sincerity and kindness just kept drawing me closer to her and the more I got to know her, the more I felt like God wanted me to learn something from her. I had stopped cleaning when I got pregnant with my third son and even after he was born, I just didn't have time. Somehow God made a way and brought me back to Cindi when Enoch was about 6 months old. I started cleaning again but this time it was more like once every month or even once every 6 weeks. Throughout that time we continued to keep in touch. To say that I am forever thankful or grateful isn't even enough.

John, Beatrice, Enoch
Daniel, Micah

Visit to Kenya

Cindi

In the early part of 2015, Beatrice and John made a huge decision to take a trip to Africa to visit their families. She asked my opinion and I'm so grateful that I didn't tell her what I really thought about the idea. I'm a very practical person when it comes to finances, so naturally I felt the money could be better spent on their current needs instead of spending so much for a trip. But they hadn't seen their families in many years, so that is what they chose to do. I'm so grateful now that they made that decision!

When they returned, Bea told me about a dream that God had put on her heart.

Beatrice

My family and I planned a trip to Kenya and Zimbabwe in 2015. It was during this visit that I realized my calling. As a child, I had always thought that one day I would help establish an orphanage home. My heart really cries out to orphans and the many challenges they encounter.

One day my father-in-law was driving down the road somewhere close to Busia, Kenya when I saw many children in school uniforms running very fast on the tarred roads. Initially I thought, "Wow, these Kenyans must really love to run." It didn't occur to me that the students who were running didn't have shoes. John, my husband, explained to me that they could not walk slowly because it was so hot and the tarred road was unbearable to walk on. Because of that, the only option was for them to run fast so as not to get their soles burnt and blistered from the heat.

It troubled me how so many children didn't even have a pair of shoes to put on when other children in America were privileged to have as many as 10 or more pairs of shoes. That did not go well with me, especially after John told me about jiggers and how many disadvantaged children get affected by jiggers to the point of not even being able to walk and go to school. I was very concerned and as we continued on our journey, the heaviness in my heart deepened.

Suddenly, a thought flashed through my mind but I ignored it - on purpose. In fact, I remember John and his dad talking about something else, but my mind was in a different place. I started thinking about how I was almost in that same situation as those kids, even though mine was short lived. My situation had a happier ending - someone had come to my rescue.

That thought did not leave me even after I came back to the US. I struggled with it so much that I had to act on it. I know God was prompting me to do something but as I looked at myself, logic told me I could not achieve it. I started telling myself that there is so much need in this world and I cannot take care of it all by myself. Yet God was telling me that in order to make a difference, you start with one person or one situation at a time. It's not like He wanted me to be superwoman and save the world from its troubles overnight.

One of my friends, Odile told me about the mud run in Omaha, Nebraska where hundreds of kids race in the mud. After the race they have tons of big trash cans where they dump the shoes they had used to race in. I thought that maybe I could go collect all those shoes, wash them in the lake, dry them and hopefully ship them to Kenya. The thought of it was overwhelming. I didn't know exactly how I was going to do it, but I didn't dismiss the thought.

A few months passed and I thought, oh well, I would love to collect used shoes but then the shipping to Kenya would be very expensive. I knew getting used shoes might not be a problem, but then shipping them was definitely an issue. Since I didn't have a job it was so easy for me to postpone the whole idea until I got one. So I told myself that I would do it once I started working – which was going to be a long while since I was a stay at home mother. I resolved that 5 years would be a good timeframe and I would pursue this dream of mine once I got settled financially.

I told my husband of this dream; how I was going to start collecting used shoes and getting them ready to ship to Kenya. Being the man that he is, he immediately showed his support and promised to help me however he could, although he did not hide his thoughts on how I was ever going to achieve it. I remember him telling me that he knew he would be the one going to the lake to wash off those muddy shoes because he knew I probably wasn't really going to do that. He was however okay with it. He just let me dream on without any discouragement. I was sure that I had finally found a purpose in my life but I kept asking God why He would put such a burden in my heart when He knew that financially I wasn't in a position to carry it out. Didn't I have my own problems to take care of? I mused.

The amazing thing about God is that His timing is perfect. He doesn't look at the impossible or the finances. When He wants His work done, He makes room for provision.

Another Dream - Cindi

Beatrice's other dream after returning home was to build her parents a home. I remember her talking about that desire years before but they couldn't afford to build one. Then after seeing the conditions her parents were living in, she decided to get a job when they returned to America. She made enough money to build them a house, a bathroom and to do a little landscaping. Victoria (her sister) built them the kitchen (which was separate from the house because they cook over a real fire).

When Beatrice had finished building the house in 2015, John lost his job. After looking for a job for several months, they finally relocated to Texas. I was sad to see them go. I also felt that the shoe idea might die or be transferred to me, but I wanted to stay open to whatever direction God would lead.

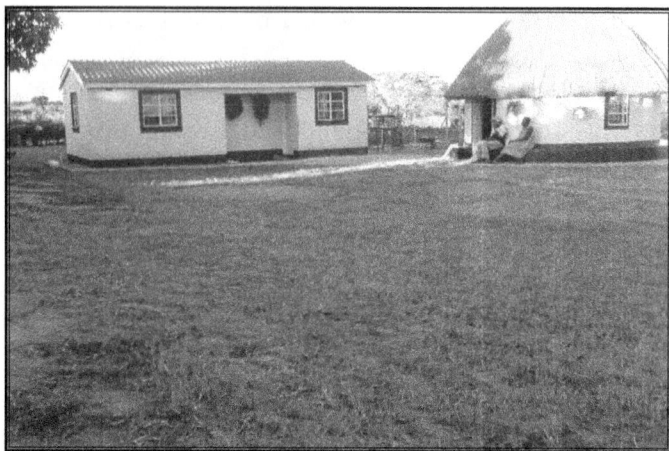

Grace and Newton's home built by Beatrice and Victoria

My Early Years

Growing up - Beatrice

I remember growing up without many pairs of shoes. To be exact, we mostly had two or three pairs of shoes at a time; one pair was a school shoe, the other pair for church and a pair of sandals for using in the bathroom. My parents were neither poor nor middle class - they were somewhere in-between. What I know as fact is that they did their best to make sure that we were educated, because education was our ticket or pass out of poverty.

In our neighborhood we were considered to be better off than other families. This wasn't because my parents were special. It was simply because they worked very hard. My father was a carpenter and he would spend weeks out in the farms doing carpentry work for the white farmers. He used to sleep outside in the fields even in harsh weather, all this as an effort to make sure that he could put food on the table for his family. I admire this quality about him to this day.

My mother, on the other hand was a very resourceful woman. She had a vegetable garden and she would spend hours working in her garden. She would then sell the vegetables and have extra money to help around the house, ensuring also that we had relishes from her garden and we would never starve. One time she had a knitting machine and she used to make sweaters and knitwear for resale. This was big business at one point. She taught me how to knit using a machine and by the time I was in 5th grade, I was a professional in knitting.

In the US most children would get paid to do chores or for helping around the house, but not in my country. It was expected of us as children to help our parents out as much as we could. This also meant no whining or complaining. We quickly learned that from a very tender age. I actually enjoyed helping my mother knit. She had that business while there was a demand for her products and after the demand decreased, she moved on to something else. She started going out of the country to buy things for resale. That business also lasted for a little while but she never stopped her vegetable garden, which remains standing and flourishing to this day.

Once a month our family used to go grocery shopping. This was one of the most glorious days of the month because that's when we would get to buy luxury foods like yogurt and ice-cream. It was once a month that we would each get a small yogurt container. After grocery shopping we would then go to a little kiosk and buy meat pies and soda. The ride back home was the peak of the day. My parents would pay for a taxi and we would load up our groceries and as we drove past the houses in our neighborhood, all the other kids would chase the taxi as we waved at them. It was as if we were celebrities because most of them had never had that experience before.

Now that I'm an adult, I see the sacrifices that my parents had to go through, all to make sure that we would be on our own feet one day. I am forever grateful for the decisions they made in their lives and most of all for them taking me in as one of their own children.

Devotion and prayer time was an everyday thing before bedtime. My father's favorite song that we used to sing almost every night had the words, *'Lord, do as You wish. Mold me, teach me the way You want me. The power is Yours, the will is Yours...'* and the other one was, *'The sun has set, stay with me Lord. Darkness has come, this time as we go to sleep, Oh Lord stay with me....'*

We always used to take turns praying every night and we would go by age. One thing I remember so well was the repetition in prayer. Victoria would say the same exact prayer I would have prayed the previous day. I'm talking about word for word. This wasn't even the Lord's Prayer, and she would literally memorize it. I think my sister would have been good in an acting career. It was hilarious and we used to love prayer time. We saw how God answered different prayers and because of that, I still stand on my faith because of my parents. That's the same principal we are using to raise our boys. It is very important to teach children about faith at a young and tender age. I am grateful that most of my family members have a relationship with Christ.

I really want to thank my parents for setting a good foundation for me. I couldn't have asked for better parents than the ones God chose for me. Our household was always one filled with laughter and love - qualities that I will treasure forever.

My Sister Chipo's Death - Beatrice

So many deaths happened in my life as I grew up; adults and kids alike, all close relatives, parents, brothers, sister, aunts, uncles, cousins, and grandparents. You can't help but get to a point where you start asking yourself if you are the next one to die. It's only hope that kept me going. Without it I could have given up.

After having me, my mother had three other daughters; Patience, her late twin sister Chipo, and then Patricia. Chipo was the older of the twins even though she was the smaller one in stature. When my biological mother would come visit us she would sometimes bring the twins with her. We would also go visit on school breaks. This gave me an opportunity to be with my mother's daughters at least once a year.

What I remember most about the twins was how fun they were to be around. Chipo was a prayer warrior and Patience a preacher. The twins started speaking at a very early age, but Chipo was sick all the time from the day she was born, and the doctors never figured out what the cause was. Patience started walking very early but Chipo could not walk due to her health condition. My mother had visited so many churches and every time she heard of a preacher who could pray for the sick, she would carry Chipo on her back and my older sister, Tsitsi, would carry Patience. Together they would walk very long distances so that Chipo could be healed.

Chipo had been prayed for by so many pastors and many hands had been laid on her head to the point that she started praying for herself even before she could speak well. Patience on the other hand would pick up any book she found and start preaching to her twin sister and then lay hands on her head and pray for her. It was so heartwarming to see both of them worship and praise God together. They would shout 'Hallelujah' and sing songs of praise.

Sometimes you wonder why God had to take Chipo away when she was only 3 ½ years old. He is the God who gives and takes away. He has plans that we would never be able to understand since we can only see part of that plan. I believe that in heaven all our questions will be answered. I stand on the hope that I will see my younger sister together with my mother and my other relatives in heaven one day.

I was almost 11 when Chipo left us. Losing a sister is such an inexplicable experience. It just doesn't add up. Why, Lord, why? What hurt me the most was watching my mother's pain. She almost didn't know what to do with herself and yet she had to be strong for her other kids. She would weep during the funeral and when Patience walked into the room, she would fake a smile. She was laid to rest but her memories were never forgotten, especially since her twin sister continued asking for her.

I know they say time heals, but the truth is, it all depends on the day. Some days are harder than others. I would imagine that there is nothing more painful than losing a child. I don't know if there is a law to life or what, but I just think that a child dying before their parents is one of the most painful things one could experience.

Chipo wasn't given much time to live and enjoy life to the fullest. But I do believe God used her to accomplish her purpose in the short time she was here on earth.

The Separation and My Mother's Death - Beatrice

During my first year of high school in June of 1998 when I was 13 years old, my biological mother thought that she was in a position to take care of me. She had met someone, remarried and had had two more daughters after myself; Patience and Patricia (actually three including Chipo). She came to take me to stay with her in June.

The separation from my siblings was very painful. I had grown to love my cousins dearly, being raised as if we had all come from the same womb. I missed them terribly. We had lived together under one roof, doing everything together for 10 years. Unfortunately, we had to say our goodbyes and I had to start yet another new life, but this time with my biological mother. The lifestyle was a little different from what I was used to so I had to adjust. One thing I am still thankful for until today is that at least God gave me a chance to stay with my mother for those six months.

Around October, my mother developed three huge boils on different parts of her body- one after the other. They were very painful. We would watch her cry and writhe in pain. The doctors didn't know what was going on. No one else could bear hearing her cry out in that much pain, but still her wounds had to be dressed. I took it upon myself to nurse her and dress the wounds. It had to be done so I would clean and dress her wounds three to four times a day.

In December of that same year she started deteriorating and we were not sure what was going on. She spent Christmas day lying down in pain. Little did we know that would be the last Christmas she would spend with us. On the 29th of December she was taken to the hospital and the doctor said she had pneumonia. She was given some pain medication and that was it. When she came back home after the doctor's visit, she asked my sister to prepare lunch for her. She never had lunch that day. I watched my mom struggle for her life. She could not breathe properly, and just like that, she took her last breath while sitting on the couch.

The thought of losing a mother never occurred to me. I always thought that I would have my mother with me forever. Now that I had lost both parents, the journey of being an orphan began. Sitting in the front yard as we watched neighbors and relatives come to the house to offer condolences, I thought to myself that surely God did not exist. Why would He have me stay with my mother for just 6 months and then she dies? Why did I even have to move? Why would He have her die and leave such young kids? I never thought that I could ever smile again in my life.

Funerals in Zimbabwe are done differently from the US. People gather around for days and close relatives can stay for weeks. After my mother died we had relatives stay with us for a while. They do this in order to console the bereaved. I know in the US that mourners only gather on the day of burial and sometimes people only meet at church and the place of burial. That will never happen in my country. In fact, in some funerals, the bereaved spend a lot of money hosting mourners. Funerals are pretty much like a big wedding that lasts for days, with the only exception that people are mourning and crying.

My two younger sisters, Patience and Patricia, were 6 and 3. Lots of emotions were going through my head. I just wondered how I was ever going to heal from losing a mother. My older sister Tsitsi and I went to stay in the rural area with my grandmother, while my aunt took Patience and Patricia to live with her. Life was very different in the rural. It was another new adventure for us.

In Zimbabwe when someone dies and leaves children behind (especially minors), the relatives have to take the children into their homes. This is what happened in our case. My older sister Emily was already married. Since there were four of us, we had to be divided unless someone could take care of all of us.

Unlike the US where children go to foster homes, get adopted, or the government comes in to help, whoever takes the children in have to do it all by themselves. They have to do this with their current income as there are no subsidies or support. It's not always the best for orphaned children because some end up getting mistreated by their own relatives. But I'm grateful to say God really took care of us in that regard.

The belongings of the deceased are distributed among the relatives. This includes clothes, furniture, kitchen utensils, etc. There isn't a Goodwill or estate sales for the average person. Some people may draft a will with instructions on what and how they would want things done after they pass. The person who takes the children is supposed to get most of the deceased person's property and "wealth" just in case they can't afford to take care of the children. That way they can sell some of the valuables should the need arise. This doesn't necessarily happen with every family though. Some family members actually fight for the belongings, especially if the deceased was very wealthy. I am so glad this type of drama didn't happen when my mother passed. Maybe that was because she wasn't wealthy.

One thing that hurt me the most when I went back to Zimbabwe was that I wasn't able to find my mother's grave. My sister Emily, her husband Tsitsi, John and I spent two hours in the graveyard trying to locate her plot. I remember my mother's grave having a tombstone, but since the city council was no longer taking care of the cemetery, we could not find it. The grass was about 6 feet tall and there were so many thorny bushes that we could hardly see anything. The sign on her grave had either been vandalized or stolen. It had been my hope that I would go visit the site, especially since more than a decade had passed. But unfortunately, it didn't happen. I was torn to pieces.

My Experience in the Rural Areas with My Grandmother - Beatrice

Sitting under a huge tree with hundreds of other students, waiting for a government official to arrive, I never thought in my wildest dreams that one day I would end up in the US. I was chosen to be one of the recipients for uniforms and a scholarship because I was an orphan; a status that did not ring true to me because as far as I was concerned, my parents were back in Chinhoyi. I never saw or imagined my life any further than that particular day.

The seven months that I stayed in the rural areas with my maternal grandmother were to be the hardest period of my life. It can only be God's grace that gave me the strength to endure the entire period. I believe

God allowed me to go through this period for a reason. My mother had just died so my grandmother had to take care of us. If there was ever a time that I lost hope it was this period. I could see a bleak future and I wondered why God had forsaken me and my biological siblings.

There was no electricity in the rural areas so we had to use firewood for cooking and keeping warm during the rainy season and winter. Since we didn't have any money, it meant that we had to go to the mountain and fetch the firewood and bring back a bundle of firewood balanced on top of our heads. We also didn't have any running water or bathroom facility on the homestead. We literally had to go use the bush for a toilet. We took baths and did laundry down at the river. It was definitely an experience I will never forget.

I thought to myself how life had changed drastically for us. This is true for anyone. Sometimes we never plan for changes. Life just happens and you cannot control anything. I am just glad that no matter where you are or what you are going through in life, God promises to be there.

My grandmother didn't have any source of income and it was very tough for her to put food on the table. Looking back at my life then, I really have a lot to thank God for. I am not saying that the people who are still living in those conditions should not thank God. In fact, the interesting thing is that they are forever grateful, even with the little they have. In life we all have different things to thank God for. While we are here in the US thanking God for the cars, the houses, the vacations we go on and some of the luxuries we have, there are people who are just thankful for the air they breathe.

Trust me, when I was staying with my grandmother I do not remember praying and specifically asking God for my life to change or to be in the US one day. Yes, I remember asking God why He had taken my mother so early, but to think that I ever imagined or dreamt that my life would be any better than it was would have been a lie. All that mattered at that time was to have food and water. There were just a lot of things that I wanted or needed at that time and listing them all would have meant I would be praying for hours and hours.

When you are really in need, that's when you realize that this life doesn't belong to you. You quit asking God for the things you need. Instead you just start praising and worshipping Him for who He is, not for what He gives to you. There is nothing wrong with asking but when you have been without for so long, you learn to pray differently.

The word hope didn't exist in my vocabulary any more. I was a young orphaned girl whose life had changed dramatically in a short space of time. I was also still so young in my Christian faith that I did not realize that God is the author and finisher of our faith and that His ultimate plan prevails – a plan that gives us a hope and a future; a hope that I had lost and a future that I did not envision.

Now in my adult life as a wife and mother, I realize that we sometimes waste our time asking God for specifics, but if that's not what He has planned for you, it will never happen. God is sovereign and He rules over all. If only we could grasp that part and know that He is in control, we would cease to worry about all of our problems. In fact His word speaks specifically about worry. In Luke 12:25, Jesus asks; *'Who of you by worrying can add a single hour to his lifespan?'*

Now I know God had not forgotten me during my stay with my grandmother. He chose for me to go through that for a reason and that's why I am writing about it now - so that other people who may have lost hope might gain it back. There is hope in Christ Jesus.

Living in that little homestead were my grandmother, my sick uncle, my sick aunt and her two children, my sister and I. The seven of us would have cornmeal mash (sadza) alone (it should usually be accompanied by a relish) for dinner. Most of the time we didn't have vegetables or meat to accompany the mash. The little water well that was at the homestead had dried up so we couldn't even have a garden due to the scarcity of water. We could only wait and rely on the rains to water our garden, and the rainy season was only a few months at the end of the year and a few months in the new year.

Bathing with soap was a luxury; we hardly had enough soap to bathe with or even to wash dishes or do laundry. I remember my sister's boyfriend Peter buying groceries for us once. It was like Christmas had come early for us because then we had soap and lotion and we could go to the river to wash our clothes and take a real bath. I will never forget that day. The smiles on everyone's faces were priceless.

My Grandmother - Beatrice

My maternal grandmother also had a tough life though she lived to be 90. She had to bury five of her own children. It was so unbearable having to watch her mourn as she buried her children. My three uncles, my aunt and my mother all died. That's when you ask God to grant you the serenity to accept the things you cannot change, the courage to change the things you can, and the wisdom to know the difference. At that point in life you almost want to give up, but my grandmother taught me one very important thing. Through all this she would say a very long prayer every night before she went to bed. She didn't know how to read, so obviously she couldn't read her Bible. But she was very good at memorizing the verses that she heard at church. What a prayerful woman she was. I really miss her.

Bea's birth mom giving her a kiss, Grace and Victoria

Move to the U.S.

Beatrice

After 7 months of unimaginable struggle, I moved back to Chinhoyi with my aunt and uncle (present day mom and dad), to finish high school. It was hard for me to adjust well in school because in a span of two years, this would have been my fourth high school. My lifestyle had obviously changed again, but it was much better now than it had been in the rural. I was forever grateful. I could somehow see light at the end of the tunnel.

In 2000, my cousin Heather came to visit us in Zimbabwe from the US. She asked about my progress in school and she promised my mom that if I did well in high school, she would help me come over to the US to attend University. That made me work very hard. I had a lot to catch up on so I did my best. My mother hired different teachers so I could go for extra lessons. Just the dream of coming to the US kept me studying. I was very grateful that Heather had offered to help me study abroad.

As was planned, I did well in high school and I was very anxious to let Heather know about my results. I sent a letter by regular mail from Zimbabwe to the US. I don't know what I was thinking because that was the poorest mode of communication, as some mail never gets sent out from Zimbabwe. I wondered why Heather had not responded, but of course she had not received the letter yet.

That's where my best friend, Onai, comes in. As I was telling her of my plans, she asked why I had not sent her an email. I was so confused. When she asked me if I had Heather's email address, I said yes, I had it. We went to an internet café where she asked for the address and I gave her a home address. She explained to me what an email was and we both laughed so hard. She helped me create an email address. Only cool people had email addresses back then. Onai helped me look for Heather online through a site called 'Gradefinder', almost similar to Facebook now.

We sent her an email and bam, she responded within a day. That's how we started communicating and after that I got accepted at the University of

Nebraska in Kearney. I came to the US in November of 2002, stayed with Heather for a while in Indiana, and then moved to Nebraska.

It only took that email and my journey began. To say I am grateful for what Heather did for me is an understatement. She helped me realize my dream - a dream that I thought had died. Only God could have made this possible. Without Him nothing is possible (at least nothing of eternal value), but with Him, *all* things are possible. I see now that God already had plans for me, even while I was busy making my own plans.

If only I had known that God had all these plans for me, maybe I would not have shed as many tears as I did back then. Of course, life always has ups and downs whether you are in the US or in Zimbabwe. It's just that for me, I never thought God had any plans for my life other than taking my mother from me and making me suffer. After my mother's funeral I never thought that I could ever smile again.

One of the reasons why we are writing this is to show that no one ever knows the plans that God has for the future. I know for sure that I probably would not have been able to feel and think of other children the way I do now. I would have been busy worrying about my own problems. I am so grateful now that I went through each of those experiences growing up. God used a time in my life when I was at my lowest point and turned it into something that's helping many children and impacting their hearts and souls, especially those who might have lost hope.

I need them to know that there is hope no matter what their circumstances are. God will show up where and when you don't even expect Him to. Just know that He knows everything that goes on in your life and trust me, He already knows the outcome. When He says 'YES' to something, no one can stop it. There is hope in Christ even when it doesn't seem or look like He is watching.

In December 2006, I got married to John Ogomo. We had met on campus when I first started college but I was still too young to even think of dating. However, we were just friends the whole time. Almost more like brother and sister because he was very protective of me. We were both still in college when we got married and now we have three wonderful boys - Daniel, Micah and Enoch.

When we were in college, God brought different people into our lives that came alongside of us. People like Pastor Bruce and Nancy Demmel, Dorothy Pio, Al and Genevieve Payne, and some whom I haven't mentioned. Some helped with part of my tuition while others offered prayers, support, encouragement, or free babysitting so I could go to school. I could never be more thankful in life. God made sure that He provided whenever provision was needed. This helped us learn to be more grateful and we quickly learned that God provides for His children and He had a purpose for us here in the US.

Several years back I had the opportunity to meet Alvin and Genevieve Payne. Alvin was a missionary to Zimbabwe for many years. He 'happened' to meet my mom during one of his trips to Africa. I got his contact information from my mother and we kept in touch. My mother had told Alvin about me and said that I lived in the US but she never gave him her name. When she told me to call him I was afraid he wouldn't know who I was talking about when I mentioned my mother. But I guess she made quite an impression on him because he remembered her.

After I got pregnant with my first son I stopped going to college. Because I now had a child, this meant I wouldn't be able to work and pay for my tuition. Alvin and Genevieve offered to loan me the money to pay for my tuition. This offer was much more than just help with tuition because not going to school would have meant that my student visa would expire and I would have had to leave the country. God showed His presence in my life again. He had set everything up and I am so glad and thankful to the Payne family that I graduated.

Sometimes I feel guilty that I haven't gotten to use my Degree as I wanted to, but Genevieve assures me all the time that I am doing the greatest job by staying home with my children, even though it doesn't have any financial benefits. I couldn't be more thankful to God for bringing such people into my life. Now I have the privilege of living only 30 minutes from them (since God moved us to Texas!) and it's my hope that I can give back the little I have, even if it's just my time.

Another time that God showed me how He was always taking care of me was when I had a car accident with my first car. John had actually bought it for me before we had started dating. I really needed a car to go to work so that I could pay for tuition and be able to stay in the US legally. The car was completely totaled. During this time I was renting a room in the Associate Pastor's basement. Pastor Mitch and his wife Melanie were very kind to me.

It was announced at church that I was involved in an accident and without much thought, a few people volunteered to raise money so they could buy me a car. The response was very overwhelming. This could have only happened because God surely had my back. They bought me a $3500 car, gave me money for registration fees and even money for gas! What more could anyone ask for? I don't know about you, but it seems to me that when God blesses and gives back, He surely does it ten times as much (or even more), considering my first car was worth only $300!

Heather and Beatrice

More Dreams

Grace's Dream - Cindi

In December of 2015, Beatrice was cleaning for one of her last times before moving. She happened to mention that she was going to send some money back home to her family and her relatives for Christmas.

I was most impressed by what her mother, Grace, did with the money she received. Instead of using it on immediate needs, she began building a chicken coop so she could raise chickens and goats for food and also to sell for income. The money was only enough for the foundation and she had no way of knowing how she would ever finish the structure. But she had a dream and she was willing to step out in faith and begin the process.

When I received a picture of the foundation, I envisioned an overgrown slab of cement that was of no use to anyone. I decided to get a quote to see what it would cost to finish the coop, along with enough funds to buy some chickens and goats (because what good is a chicken coop if you can't afford to buy chickens?). We determined to go ahead with the project to bring it to completion.

Grace was so excited! She left me a voice message thanking me and telling me that I should come for a visit. I laughed at the thought of it and told Beatrice that would never happen! (I caution you city girls to be careful when using the word 'never'!)

After that project was completed, we thought it would be fun to do some type of 'blessing bag' there (like I mentioned in a previous chapter) but I wasn't sure how that would look. I knew something had to be different this time because it would be very hard to give someone who had literally nothing, $5.00 to give away to someone else. So we determined to give them two $5 bills with the instructions to keep one and give one away.

I had also just finished writing the book "YOLT" so we came up with the idea to give the book along with the money. That way they would not only receive money but also hear about God's love for them.

We sent letters over to be printed and found someone going to Zimbabwe who could deliver the books and cards. Bea's sister, Victoria, offered to be in charge of the distribution process. We sent books to her and wired the cash to complete the packets.

I have to laugh because Victoria told Beatrice that she didn't think it was a very good idea to do this. But once she got started, my theory proved true. She was hooked on giving! Her husband, Kumbi, also wanted to get involved in the distribution.

They reported back with pictures of people they had given them to, along with the stories of these people. I remember being told of one man who said his family hadn't eaten in two days! I'm pretty sure he kept all of the money he received.

They were also instructed to read the book and pass it on with the second $5.00. I have no idea what happened to most of the money and books that were sent, but I'd like to tell you where some of it ended up.

Another Move - Beatrice

Now going back to my dream – after we came back from Kenya my husband lost his job. We somehow knew that it was going to happen because of some workplace politics. He started his job search in July 2015 but he could not find anything in Omaha. John eventually got a job in Texas! It was an amazing opportunity for him but my heart was really torn because Omaha, Nebraska had become our home. This is where we had lived for the past 7 years and we had made such strong relationships. It was indeed sad to leave but we believed God had called us to move to Texas, even though we knew there were certain things about Nebraska that we were going to miss. One thing for sure I knew I wasn't going to miss was the harsh winters. Otherwise, I was going to miss my friends, family, the environment, Lifegate church and much more.

A few weeks before I left I went to Cindi's to clean. We had a deep heart to heart talk and she asked me if we would ever come back to Nebraska. I felt the connection even though neither of us mentioned it. It was at that moment that I realized I was going to miss her terribly. She had actually become like my second mother. I never knew until then how close we had become and how the attachment was greater than I anticipated. Though I didn't cry, I told her that we would come back to visit and we would visit her too. She told me how much she was going to miss my cleaning her house and when I went back home, I told my husband how hurt I was for not being able to be there for Cindi anymore. However, God still had a plan.

I went back to clean again before her Christmas party. We were just chatting and we discussed about Christmas, my family, my visit to Kenya, Zimbabwe and my experience. I also shared photos of my parent's house that Victoria and I had built for them. She was very impressed and I ended up sharing with her my "crazy shoe idea". Right away Cindi said that she was going to help me with the shipping costs even after I had told her how expensive the shipping was going to be. I was very hopeful and grateful that at least someone believed in me so much that they would even consider investing their money in my dream.

My phone rang just as we were talking and it was a message from Zimbabwe. Apparently a friend had sent me a photo of my mother standing in her garden. I then showed the photo to Cindi and she asked why the garden had a grass fence. I told her it was because the animals would eat the vegetables if left unfenced. Trust me, that photo of my mother opened up a door that no man can shut. It was literally blessing after blessing. If you don't call that investing in someone, I don't know what to call it. Cindi has invested so much in me. She took my idea and my dream as if it were her own. She never questioned why I wanted to do it or when I wanted to do it. She made the impossible become possible. I didn't even believe in my dream the way she did. I kept on cleaning as Cindi was picking things up around the house as she always did.

She also wanted to know more about my mother's chicken coop. At that time only the foundation to the coop was done so she asked me how much it would cost to finish it all up. She thought about it for a few days and then we sent the funds to my mother for the project to continue. I thought Cindi had done so much for my family and for me, but it was only the beginning. She went on to ask about what project the church could do. We both thought about it separately. I had no idea when she asked me but I thought maybe a community garden would do and then she had the same idea too. I did all the research for the garden and the fence. The people were very excited and the church ladies started planting the garden right away.

The Blessings Begin

Bathrooms for the Church - Cindi

When the blessing bags were handed out at a church service, the pastor who was there at that time suggested that if the people put in half their money ($5.00), they could build a bathroom for the church. As of that time they had a hole in the ground that they dreamt of someday building a bathroom on.

After some discussion, they all agreed to the pastor's suggestion. But then someone else got up and suggested that if they put in the whole amount ($10.00) they could build two bathrooms. That took a little more convincing because that meant they would have to give up all of the money. After much consideration they finally agreed to the plan.

But it didn't stop there. One man got up and offered 2,000 bricks for the project. You need to realize that he wasn't just going to the store to buy bricks. He had to make them. Then another man offered to do the same. Others offered to haul supplies that were available for free but they just needed a way to get them there. The women helped by carrying pails of water on their heads so the men could make cement.

When it was all finished, they ended up with three toilets – one for the men, one for the women, and a guest bathroom (which was the only one with a toilet seat made out of cement – the others were just a hole in the ground). The bathroom also had two rooms for them to take 'bucket showers'.

The people from the church worked together to make the bathrooms a reality. The builder, John, offered his services for a small fee. At one point he had to go home to finish some projects he was working on so the people went along to help him finish so that he could get back sooner. That may not sound like a big deal to us but it's a really big thing over there. Up to this time, people pretty much looked out for themselves.

When the project was almost completed, they had a celebration feast. They did a ribbon cutting on the bathroom and the women made food for everyone.

The bathrooms played a big part in bringing the community together.

Beatrice

The church members decided they were going to use that money to build a toilet since they didn't have a toilet on their church compound. This was such a blessing because the church had dug a hole for the toilet and it had been sitting there for months because they didn't have money to buy the building materials. The congregation had to use the neighbor's outhouse/toilet and you can imagine how inconvenient that might have been, considering the church has more than 150 members. Two church members said they were going to donate bricks, some were going to get river sand from the river, others said they would donate their labor and help the builder, and some of the ladies were to bring water from the borehole for building.

The whole community came together as a united force. This was so amazing because now they had the money to purchase the supplies that they could not have afforded, especially bearing in mind the economic turmoil Zimbabwe is currently going through. It was truly God's hand working in all of this.

Cindi was very touched that the church chose to invest in the house of the Lord regardless of how needy they were (the country is currently experiencing a severe drought). She said it was very thoughtful of them to do such a humble, honorable act.

After the toilet was built we thought it would be fun for the congregation to have a celebration party and boy, did they have a blast or what. They had meat- lots of meat, soda and "Christmas feast" foods which they don't normally eat on a regular basis.

A well was also needed on the church compound because there was no water there. The church people did the digging and the construction of that too. They seemed to enjoy having projects to work on and the sense of pride which came from their accomplishments.

More Projects - Cindi

When the bathrooms were done, we tried to think of more projects we could do to help the people. The area had been affected by a drought so there wasn't much food available. We decided to see if they wanted to plant a community garden. They loved the idea and worked together to make it happen.

The garden required a fence to keep the animals out. Water was also needed so Bea's mother offered to have it put in on their property since they already had a well. Several women come daily to help water and care for it.

The next project the people did was a well for the church. We were also hoping they could build the pastor a house so she could live closer to the people in the congregation but some government officials came and stopped that process until some issues were worked through.

Beatrice

We now have an update regarding the clearance for this project. They were given the permission to build and the process has begun (it may even be done by the time you are reading this). It was a long process. There were some issues with the plan. Initially they thought that they could just make up a simple plan, but then the city council said that the house was to be constructed with the same standards as if it was in the city because it was a public building.

While they were still figuring out about the plan, the congregation was busy making bricks, collecting sand from the river and also stones and little rocks from the mountain. By the time the plan was approved, all the materials that were needed had been gathered. It was also amazing how God provided money for the congregation to purchase all the remaining materials, as well as pay the labor for the builder.

Pastor Gandi and Grace arranged for the congregation to work in groups of 10 at a time to help the builder so that he wouldn't have to hire extra help. That way they all got to have a part in the construction process. They have sent many photos from Zimbabwe and it is amazing how even the women were making the bricks with mortar. You can just see how their faces are gleaming with joy as they partner together in Christ. When God wants His work done, He sure does make a way. We can't wait to see the finished project!

Grace's chicken coop

The bathroom at the church in Rusape

Shoe Dream
Becomes a Reality

Shoes for Kenya - Cindi

So back to the shoe project...I was sitting quietly one Sunday morning and I felt like God impressed on me the idea of shoes for Kenya. I was getting excited just thinking about it and I couldn't wait to call Beatrice.

I believe it was January of 2016. I was trying to think who might be having a birthday soon so they could ask people to donate shoes that we could send to Kenya. Then I got to thinking that my birthday is in February so I decided I would do the asking.

I called Beatrice to tell her my idea. She said that her birthday is also in February so we decided to both ask our friends and family to donate shoes for our project. I had flyers made up and e-mailed everyone I could think of. One of the schools several of my grandkids go to also let them ask their classrooms for shoes. All of my family and friends were great help in collecting shoes.

In a very short time we had bought and collected around 500 pairs of shoes! I had a feeling that would be the easy part. Now we had to figure out how to get them to Kenya!

Beatrice

On the other hand, Cindi was working on the shoe project. Initially we were going to get donations of used shoes. We got some donations of both new and used shoes. It was such a blessing to see how people responded to this whole shoe drive. We still didn't have enough shoes because our target was 500 pairs, so we each bought some more shoes so we could have enough. It really all started as a joke - at least to me, but then that joke would not leave me so it transformed itself into a dream. And the dream eventually came true.

Cindi asked me about what else needed to be done and I had no idea. I started researching more about jiggers as I was not quite familiar with this parasite. I would find out that jiggers were usually female parasites found mostly in tropical and sub-tropical climates that burrow their way under the skin, mostly soles, and lay eggs that later hatch to cause infection, swelling, irritation, and severe blisters to mention a few. If untreated, the parasite can lead to secondary infections that can be fatal. I contacted a few people and we purchased some supplies to take to Kenya. We also bought more supplies with donated funds that we purchased in advance. These were already in Kenya when we arrived for the anti-jigger campaign.

Cindi

Beatrice was checking into every way she could think of to get the shoes to Kenya. We finally decided that I would get them to her in Texas and we would send them by ship. It sounded like a great plan…at least until we realized that someone had to be on the receiving end when they arrived!

I didn't realize that Beatrice was thinking about going there by herself to meet the ship when it arrived. When she told me that, I said that I would think about going with her. If we shipped the shoes we wanted to do it by the end of February and we were quickly approaching that date. The shoes would take two to three months to arrive.

Towards the end of February Beatrice came up with another idea. She suggested that we take the shoes in suitcases with us. As we were figuring out how to take all those shoes by ourselves, God brought two other people along - my son, Nick, and my friend Mary, who wanted to join us on our trip. We were very excited because now we would have enough room to bring shoes *and* our clothes in the suitcases!

I was amazed that anyone would want to go on a trip like that. I didn't consider it a 'vacation'. It was more like a mission trip where you knew you could encounter some pretty hard things.

I told Beatrice that if we were going all the way to Africa, we needed to not just do the shoe distribution in Kenya but also go to Zimbabwe to see the projects that had been completed by the people there.

As I considered if this was really what God wanted me to do, He gave me very clear answers. He even seemed to speak to my fears about bathrooms and showers (I was afraid that we wouldn't have real bathrooms while we were there and city girls need their bathrooms!) He also told me to go NOW and not to put it off. Because of the things He was showing me, I kept moving forward. One of the scriptures God gave me was Psalms 67.

"O God, in mercy bless us; let Your face beam with joy as You look down at us. Send us around the world with the news of Your saving power and Your eternal plan for all mankind. How everyone throughout the earth will praise the Lord! How glad the nations will be, singing for joy because You are their King and will give true justice to their people! Praise God, O world! May all the peoples of the earth give thanks to You. For the earth has yielded abundant harvests. God, even our own God, will bless us. And peoples from remotest lands will worship Him."

The Adventure Begins

Beatrice

Now the journey to Africa was something Cindi had never dreamt of. In fact, she thought it was meant for other people but she found herself actually wanting to go. I have no idea what prompted her to do that. It had to be God. I wasn't even sure if taking Cindi to Kenya and Zimbabwe was what God had planned for us. I struggled with it a bit because I was worried for her safety and if everything was going to go as planned and how she would adjust even if it was only for a few days. But I still left it all in God's hands. When Cindi's son Nick said he was coming with us I felt so much peace, and when Mary joined the group, it was even more perfect. We were just a perfect team, handpicked by God. We could not have asked for more or less for that matter.

The plane tickets to Kenya and Zimbabwe got purchased. The dream was finally in motion. As God's agents and representatives, we were ready! As ready as we were, the possibility of complications didn't leave my thoughts. I would worry about so many things and think of everything that could possibly go wrong. I remember asking myself these kinds of questions; What if we get lost in Kenya? What if we get robbed? What if my team gets sick? Did we make enough preparations? Was I even a leader? What if no one comes to get us at the airport? What about immigration and all the luggage we had brought? Is the weather going to be okay? There were a lot of "what if" questions that I was dealing with.

I was pretty much in my own "what if" world. Had it not been for my niece, Carol, who spoke sense into me and encouraged me, I might have lost it. She assured me that God was in control and I couldn't have been able to do anything to change any of those things that I was worrying about. We prayed together and she told me that it was all going to be okay. Carol is one of the most encouraging, positive, self-driven people I know. She completely dismisses her own problems and goes out of her way to help others. This particular day she hadn't even slept, regardless of the fact that her time zone is six hours ahead of ours. As a cancer survivor, she has learned to be there for others and she has definitely been there for me.

Cindi

The dream became real when we purchased our tickets and got our many shots. Before we knew it, it was April and time to leave on our adventure. We had a few glitches along the way. The sitter Beatrice had for her boys (they now had three) fell through because of other commitments, but she was able to find a place for them while John was at work.

Bea was flying to Omaha to join us on our first flight. She went to the airport in Dallas early in the morning and her flight was delayed because of thunderstorms. She finally made it to Omaha just about two hours before we were scheduled to leave.

Mary took her first malaria pill and got sick. We asked people to pray for her and she recovered within hours! And she never had another problem with them after that. The flights were about 24 hours each way and I was surprised at how quickly they went by. Mostly we slept and ate (they fed us very well and very often on the planes)!

We had been warned that customs could decide to charge for the baggage we were bringing in to the country. It just depended on what they felt like doing at the time (or the moment). When we arrived in Nairobi, we went through customs and were only charged $142.00 in fees. We willingly paid the fee (since they started out wanting $400.00) and headed off to start our adventure.

A Dream Becomes a Reality

Bunyala, Africa - Cindi

Our first stop was Bunyala. Fred (John's brother) met us at the airport – several times- to make sure we had what we needed. He was a huge blessing to us.

We met so many wonderful people along the way. We had no idea what we were doing when we made our plans, but God knew that and He had so many people in place to help us accomplish just what we had set out to do. They were so organized that they made us look really good.

The first site we visited was Bunyala School. We were amazed at how many people were there! The room was full and there were more people outside.

The children from the schools represented did presentations for us. Some sang and danced, others recited poems. That was definitely a highlight. Then they presented us with gifts. We noticed that their uniforms were pretty tattered and worn.

Clement and Emily (John's parents) were the official organizers for Bunyala and the shoe distribution. They arranged for us to visit three sites with shoes and to offer treatment for jiggers. Deborah (Bea's sister-in-law) seemed to be in charge of the treatment. She is a pediatrician in Africa. Her daughter, Nadia (7 years old at the time), helped pass out shoes, juice and cookies.

Deborah brought Matoke (his name is the same as the name for a mashed banana dish they make there so I called him "Banana Man"- that was easier to remember!), and Fred to assist her. In all, about 70 people (both young and old) were treated for jiggers that day. Deborah said that's the most people they have treated in one day, even at the hospital. Some of the people didn't come forward to be treated because, if you have jiggers, you may be looked upon similar to someone who has leprosy.

We also passed out juice and cookies at the sites. One of the men asked the children when the last time was that they had received this kind of treat.

Some said 'never' and many couldn't remember the last time.

Mary and Nick were heartbroken because they ran out of shoes before all the children had received them. One classroom waited patiently while the other students received shoes and then there weren't enough for them. Their names and sizes were taken and someone told us about a shoe warehouse in town. We went there the next day and purchased shoes (140 more pairs) for these children (plus some extras). We were able to buy them for $2.50 a pair. We decided that if we do the shoes again, we would buy them there instead of hauling so many all the way to Africa.

Mary had been given a gift of money right before we left town. She knew she wanted to use it for something special along the way and when we went to buy the extra shoes, the cost was about $3.00 less than the money she had received! God is so good!

The teachers there make about $200.00 a month. I realize that the cost of living is less there but that still isn't much money to live on. Clement was in the process of building duplex homes where teachers could live for $45.00 a month.

Clement gave a speech at the assembly and when he addressed the parents, he told them to "Go hungry, go naked, but send your kids to school." We laughed about their 'school motto', but as we shared it with people from Africa, they weren't laughing. They wholeheartedly agreed. It made me realize that they see education as their only way out of poverty. Many of them will do all they can to help others in their family get an education. That's why so many come to America and send money home. Their sense of 'family' really spoke loudly to me.

When we were leaving Bunyala, we were stopped by the local police. They wanted to see our passports. They were going through them one page at a time very slowly. I was wondering what they could possibly be looking for. We learned later that they were hoping for a bribe. Since we weren't catching on, they finally gave them back.

As we drove through the towns I saw a few interesting things. There was a young man with a load of lumber strapped to his bicycle. I also saw a man with a couch tied to his motorbike. Many people were selling their wares (fruits, vegetables, clothing and a large variety of things) along the side of the road.

In the rural motels we stayed at in Kenya they had mosquito nets around the beds. We were blessed to not have any problems with bites of any kind. We stayed healthy and were accident free the entire trip.

Bunyala

Clement and Emily

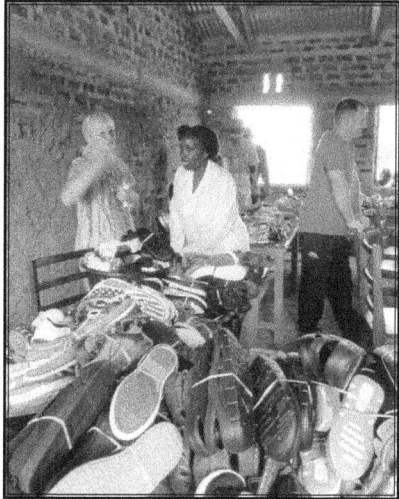

Cindi, Deborah and Nick at shoe distribution.

School assembly for shoe distribution.

Deborah

Presentation by some of the students.

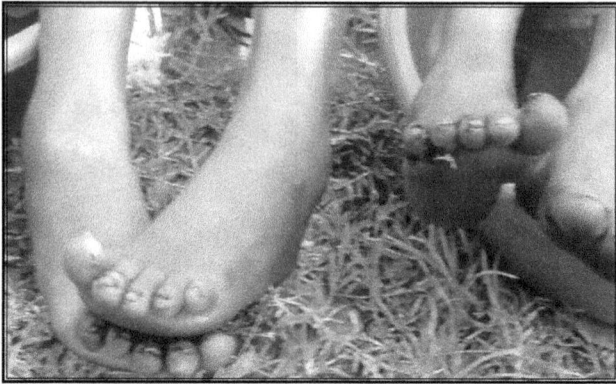

jigger treatment

More jigger treatment

Nick, Fred, Cindi, Matoke, Mary and Beatrice

Bunyala

Rusape, Africa - Cindi

Our next big stop was Rusape. Kumbi and Victoria were our drivers for this part of the trip. Victoria told us that they had recently moved to another location just so they would have more room for us to stay! They also graciously gave up their beds for us (a custom there) while they slept on couches and the floor.

I had a chance to thank Victoria for distributing the blessing bags. Instead she thanked me for allowing them to do it. It made her see how blessed they truly were and caused her to see others differently. On Christmas Eve, they went through their clothes and took some of them to homeless people. She said it was the best Christmas they ever had.

The next day we arrived at Grace and Newton's lovely home (the one Beatrice and Victoria had built for them). Grace did most of the planning in Rusape. We were greeted by many of Bea's relatives and friends with a song of welcome and a huge sign they had made. It was a great start to our next adventure. I can't remember a time when I've ever felt so welcome!

I was impressed by many of the women. They have nothing but they love to sit around (or dance) and sing praises to God for who He is to them and for

His blessings. They realize that life is about so much more than what they possess at the present time. I believe they see the hope of what is to come. And they know that God is with them through every step of the process. When life is toughest, they don't lose their faith. It only grows stronger.

We got the grand tour when we arrived. It was so fun to see the projects they had finished like the chicken coop, the garden (it was doing very well), the bathrooms and the well. Grace had someone make us dresses that were beautiful. Nick was given a shirt that was very nice also.

We stayed in a motel not too far away. We also got a room for Kumbi and Victoria. She protested saying we didn't need to do that. When I asked her where they would sleep if we didn't get them a room, she said they planned to sleep in the car. She told Beatrice that she had never stayed in a motel before.

At one point, Nick had to go to the store in Rusape for supplies. An employee there went to find something for him and he was concerned that they might not remember who they had been helping. Then he had a good laugh as he realized that he was the only white person in the whole store (and probably in the whole area!). I guess he was so comfortable there that it didn't feel like he was the only white person around.

Another time when we were in town, I felt I was getting low on cash and we tried to find an ATM machine where we could get more money. We tried several but had no success. The reason they weren't working was because they were out of cash. The country goes through these shortages often and when they do, the people are unable to get money.

So much that we saw was like stepping back in time. We saw things that most Americans would never dream of – like the fact that there are no indoor bathrooms or electricity in many of the homes. It's a totally different lifestyle than what we are used to. But because their lifestyle is so much simpler, the people don't share the same stresses that we Americans do. They live at a much slower pace than the people in our culture do. Their biggest concern is having enough food to eat.

When we arrived at church the next day, the people gave us the red carpet treatment. They were laying down pieces of fabric ahead of us to walk on. The church service lasted about 4 ½ hours and it amazed me that most of the women sat on the ground during the entire service. The seats are mostly for the men. I thought of a typical service in America. People have a hard time sitting on padded seats for much more than one hour. I can't imagine what would happen if church lasted over four hours on seats that looked very uncomfortable!

The children watched us closely. I'm pretty sure they were fascinated by our skin color (since we were definitely in the minority). I shook many of their hands and they seemed to like that. It made me wonder how Jesus must have felt when the children wanted to come near to Him. He loved them, and after seeing how the children responded to us, I can see why He did.

After the service we were able to provide the people from the church and neighboring villages with a meal. It included meat which they don't get very often. I know that God gave us the idea to do the meal. When we presented to them what we were thinking, we found out that they were getting a new pastor and they wanted to do a celebration with food.

When the congregation was asked what they had to contribute to the meal, all they could come up with were two chickens. They were going to feed the pastor and the Bishop and the people would get nothing. When we called, they decided to move the celebration back two weeks until we arrived so we could bless them.

The people showered us with gifts again. We all had a good laugh when they gave us a goat (which we named Billy)! They also gave us two big stalks of bananas, beans and a basket. We had to leave Billy with Grace since we didn't think the airline would appreciate it if we brought a goat on the plane!

We had Victoria purchase 400 bags of corn meal (which is their primary source of food) before we arrived. It was stored in a small shack and several men stayed with it all night so no one would take it.

In the afternoon, the people were organized by groups for the food distribution. They were so grateful to receive it. With the drought, many of them were running low on food. One lady who was raising her grandchildren (her children had died) thanked us and said they had not eaten in three days! Can you even imagine that? I think how many times in American we hear the phrase "I'm starving!" But for the most part we have no idea what it would be like to go without food for days.

Another man said "You have brought light to the community." I felt like we gave them hope. We were able to bless almost 400 families with food. It was such a great feeling to know they would have something to eat for at least a few weeks. I just wish we had been able to do more.

The government doesn't help the people where we visited. We were told that something like this had never happened there before (giving out shoes, treatment and food). Newton told me three times that he was "so happy"! It made my day to see him smile! He was so proud of Beatrice.

On our last day there we all went through our bags to see what clothes and supplies we could leave behind. We had each brought things that we intended to leave there. I had bought quite a few clothes on clearance for that purpose. I was going to wear them and then give them away, but when we arrived, they weren't quite right for the temperatures. So when I was ready to give them away, many still had the tags on them. I thought they might enjoy getting brand new clothes, but instead they were disappointed that we had not worn them first. That was pretty humbling. I wonder how many of us would rather have hand-me-downs instead of something new.

I was very impressed by the fact that these dear people have so little, but so many of them do all they can to take care of others in their family (even their extended family) by sending them to school or just helping them keep food on the table. Even if they happen to move to another country, many of them continue to send money home to their parents or to their families.

There is a very high rate of unemployment in Zimbabwe so Victoria went back to school for a teaching degree. She thought that she would have a better chance at becoming a teacher than anything else. Since having a maid was getting too costly, she had to leave her two children with her mother (Grace) for about four months or more. Having a maid in Zimbabwe is not as expensive as it is here in the US. A live-in maid gets paid about $60 to $80 a month, but with the economy the way it is, that's a lot of extra money to pay out every month.

Victoria said she and Kumbi would go visit the children about once a month. It was very hard for her to leave them. I wondered how I would handle that if I were in her situation. As a mother of small children, I can't imagine how it would feel to leave your children for a long period of time.

Beatrice

While making all the other arrangements, Cindi asked me what type of gifts or presents we could get for the people in Zimbabwe. I seriously had no idea but I remembered that my mother had told me about the drought they were experiencing. I somehow thought cornmeal was a bit too much so I was hesitant to tell her, considering the cost. However I thought I would give it a shot. I told her about the cornmeal and right away she said it was a perfect idea. Great minds surely do think alike. We had 400 bags of cornmeal purchased in advance for Zimbabwe, but still her heart was not settled.

She told me that she was thinking of having a meal for them while we were there and that's exactly what I was thinking too. Apparently the church was already planning on having a groundbreaking ceremony but they didn't have enough food for the celebration. So they changed their date to match up with when we would be there. This was God's provision right there because they had discussed it in church about what they were to do since there wasn't enough food for everyone and God heard their prayers.

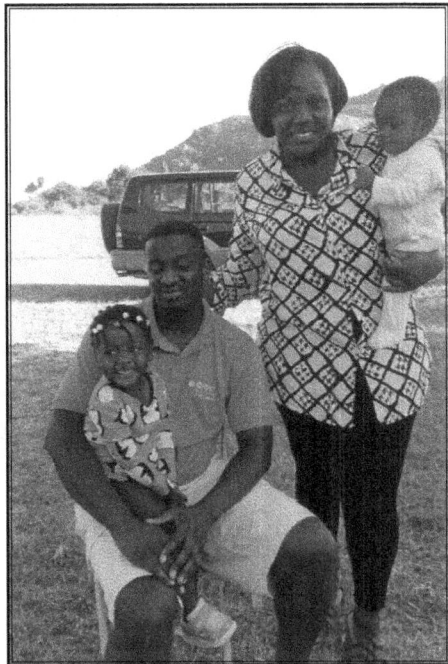

Kandy, Kumbi,
Victoria and Kudzi

*Welcome sign
in Rusape*

Grace and Cindi

Mary in Grace's garden

Bea's family

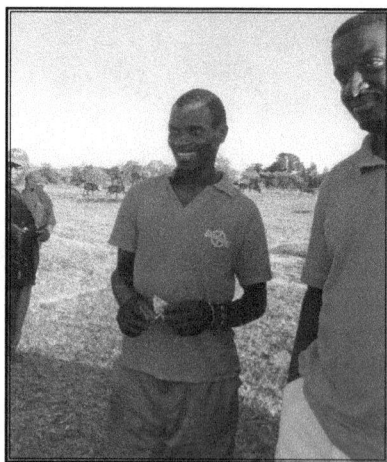

John (the builder) and Kumbi

Stella, Newton, Grace and Cindi

The church in Rusape

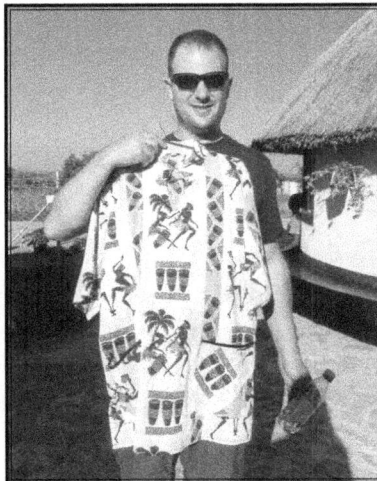

Nick with his African shirt

Inside the church with benches and seating on the ground

Cindi, Grace and Blessing with church bathroom in the background

Church service in Rusape

Children outside the church service

Assembly for food distribution in Rusape

How water is transported

Presentation of gifts (goat) after the service – Our African dresses

Children from the church

This is how Africans carry their loads

Preparing for food distribution

Line of church members and community coming for food

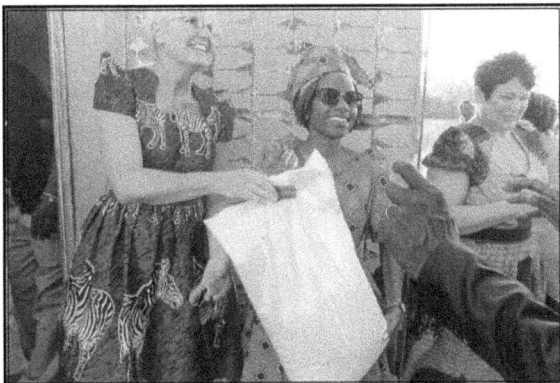

Cindi, Beatrice and Mary handing out food

Customs

I'd like to share a few of the customs we observed in Africa.

Beatrice

Breathing the same air that I used to breathe as a child brought back many childhood memories, though I had a hard time picturing myself ever doing certain things as a child. We sat in the car during one of our drives in Zimbabwe as my younger sister, Victoria, and I shared our childhood stories with Cindi, Mary and Nick. They quickly learned that a car seat is not a requirement in Zimbabwe. It is more of a luxury. Depending on how many people are riding in a car, most children just sit on someone's lap so there is enough room in the car for everyone. It was such a great time we had.

Cindi

When we sat down for a meal, they brought around a bowl, hand soap and a pitcher of water. They knelt down beside us and had us wash our hands. It was very honoring (and humbling for us).

Guests are put in a separate room to eat their meals. It seemed like all they did was cook for us and I was wondering if we were ever going to get a chance to visit with them. We were also told that they aren't supposed to talk while they are eating (and not just because their mouths are full!). I have to say that this wasn't one of my favorite customs. I would have rather spent time eating with them which would have given us more time to interact and get to know them better.

I already mentioned the one about giving up their beds. Each place we visited, they commented that we should be staying with them (since we were staying in motels). They feel honored when they can share their homes with guests (especially Americans).

Victoria mentioned several times that she was going to have a wedding. I thought that was strange since she was already married and had two children. I asked Beatrice why she was having a wedding. Her answer surprised me.

In their culture, when a man wants to marry a woman, he talks to her parents and they determine a 'bride price' so he can marry her. The groom can pay this off over time if needed. Once the price is agreed upon, they are 'married'. Most of the time, this bride price doesn't involve a wedding. Victoria has always dreamed of having a real wedding so she is hoping to have one in the near future. I also learned that Beatrice never got to have a wedding reception either.

When Victoria told me how much her wedding would cost, I again asked Beatrice how they could afford that expense. She informed me that when you announce a wedding, people usually offer to help with some part of the celebration – like maybe the pictures, the food, the dress or whatever they can afford. That way the couple is only left with part of the expense.

Beatrice

I also remember when we were in Zimbabwe at the airport. Cindi asked me why my sister Victoria was planning a wedding ceremony when she had already been with her husband for 4 years. What they didn't know was that according to the Zimbabwean culture, Victoria and her husband Kumbi were considered to be married. In Zimbabwe and many other African countries, bride price is considered to be more important than a white wedding.

Bride price is when a man brings cows and money to the bride's parents and in exchange, he gets a wife. It's supposed to be a token to the bride's parents as a thank you for raising their daughter well. The bride's parents get to charge what they think is fair to both parties, but most of the time an educated girl is worth more than a girl who has little or no education. This is because parents would have spent so much money educating their daughter and they feel that once that daughter is married, she might not be able to take care of them the same as she would if she was not married. Culturally a father's wealth is measured by how many daughters he has, because when his daughters get married, that's an opportunity for him to get cows, and cows are a sign of wealth.

Even though many couples will celebrate by having a white wedding, you cannot skip the bride price because that will be considered disrespectful to your parents. In my situation, my husband got to pay the bride price. We didn't have a big white wedding celebration. Instead Pastor Bruce and Nancy married us and we only had 9 guests.

Beatrice

Where I come from, education is highly regarded as the one tool that can give you a chance to realize your dreams. This is why today there are numerous nonprofit organizations promoting and calling for equal access to education for the girl child. The strong belief is that education brings emancipation and by getting themselves an education and thriving careers, the girls will not have to rely on a man for survival as had been the case for women such as my biological mother.

Because of the cultural emphasis on education, my parents resolved to take us to one of the best schools in Chinhoyi. It wasn't in our neighborhood or even close to where we lived. They believed that we would get a better education at that school than at the cheaper ones in our neighborhood. This school was a bit expensive but they were determined we were all going to learn there. They struggled all the way through our high school years. Three of us were in high school at the same time, which made it worse as far as school fees and school expenses were concerned. This was very hard for my parents but they soldiered through it.

My mother would always make sure that we had enough food to pack for our school lunches even though we might not have had meat to eat for dinner. Meat was very expensive, especially beef. We never lacked vegetables though since she had a vegetable garden. I remember when we would go vegetarian for about a month or so, all because we had to save money to buy something important. We used to hate it but looking back now, I'm grateful we did that. It was actually very good for our health.

We never lacked in anything that we needed for school. Education was the priority for my parents, and they would go without so much just to make sure that we had enough for school. It was such a huge sacrifice they had to make. They obviously wanted us to have a much better life than they had growing up. My mother was very intelligent but she never got a chance to finish school. Her parents were very poor so she only attended school until 7th grade. She however told herself that she would make sure that all her children got the privilege she never had. She asked God and He gave her the desire of her heart. She married a hardworking man and together they did all they could to educate their children.

I couldn't have been more grateful. Not only did they provide for their own kids but we always had relatives staying with us. Most of them were disadvantaged but my parents would help them out one way or another. My mother taught me to have a heart for others. If my memory serves me well, as far as I can remember, my parents took care of at least twenty relatives. They all stayed with us for a period of as little as two months, or even up to years at different times in our childhood.

What they did through their kindness to others taught me at a very young age to share the little that I have, even though it's not always easy to have a heart for others. That's one thing I know was modeled in my life as a child. Then when I became an adult I met different people who have shown me how to love without boundaries.

My father had a very old truck and he would drop us off at school most of the time. Because most parents at our school had fancier cars, other children were dropped off in front of the school office. Because of the condition of my father's truck, we would ask him to drop us at the gate. I remember him asking us why he had to drop us that far away and we told him that the school principal had changed the drop off rules. Little did he know that the actual reason was that we were very embarrassed by that old truck of his. The doors didn't even work. It made a lot of noise and it would produce so much exhaust smoke. Both he and his truck were simply "not cool" enough for us to be seen coming out of. So we resolved that in order for us to have a peaceful day at school, we were better off walking than having him drop us off.

With such a strong emphasis on education, you can imagine how my parents felt when in one school term I underperformed. In my family, a very high bar had been set as a standard as far as education was concerned. In this particular instance, I was 5th place in my 3rd grade class and I got a spanking that I remember in detail to this day. After that spanking I told myself that I would perform exceptionally well in school and my permanent class position after this incident was 1st, 2nd or 3rd. This was to be a trend from junior school until I graduated from high school.

Looking back in hind sight, I remain grateful to my parents for striving to give us the best education that they could afford. Today I have an accounting degree from the University of Nebraska, while my sister Victoria graduated from a Zimbabwean university with a degree in Tourism Management. My baby brother Tanya did us all proud when he scooped the highest score in his high school exams and is now studying pre-medicine at the same college where I attended in the US.

Tuition Costs for Education in Bunyala and Rusape

Tuition costs vary by region in both Zimbabwe and Kenya. Rural tuition costs are cheaper than in the city. The cost also depends on the facilities that the school offers and this applies to both government and private schools. In Bunyala and Rusape where we visited, tuition ranges from about $150 to $210 per year and this doesn't include uniforms. Almost all schools have a uniform policy. This is to insure that all students look the same regardless of their social status. This may not sound like it's a lot of money but when the economy struggles, so do most parents. This causes them to struggle to send their children to school.

Most parents in the rural are not employed. They survive on subsistence farming which means they have to sell their crops and animals so they can send their children to school. The children also get to help with the farming and taking care of the animals. It's more like a family business but without much profit.

The disadvantage of relying on farming to send children to school is that if a child isn't getting good grades, parents quickly pull the child out of school and they never get the chance to get educated. Animals such as cattle, goats and sheep are a sign of wealth. The more you have, the wealthier you are. With this mentality, parents don't want to waste money on a child who will not benefit them.

Some families are blessed to have relatives who work in the city or maybe some that might have left the country. These relatives many times help with tuition costs so that it's not such a burden on the parents. And bear in mind that most people have many kids so the costs do add up.

You can imagine the pressure that most students have to deal with; having to maintain a certain grade average so they can continue going to school. It is worse for girls than for boys; some parents believe that if a girl child isn't performing well in school then she needs to get married so they can get bride price in the form of cows. But in reality, bride price only takes care of short term problems. However, out of a poverty mindset, many parents choose bride price over their daughter's education.

Lack of hope might also make some teenage girls elope or cause them to stay with a man even without him paying the bride price. And to make matters worse, not all of those marriages flourish. Some might end in divorce with children now added to the equation, while others might not even make it in life because of HIV. It's so easy to judge others when one is not in that situation, but I have to admit that I myself actually had the thought of getting married as a teenager while I was staying with my grandmother.

We do take hope for granted at times but lack of it can make anyone have unimaginable thoughts, thoughts one would barely think of in their right mind. I remember thinking to myself if there would ever be anything else for me to do in life. I could barely see or think of my future. So as I looked at most of those children during my trip (and especially the girls), my prayer was that they would not lose hope and that God might give them direction in their lives because I know what it feels like to be where they are.

There are also a lot of orphans who stay with relatives or grandparents, but it isn't just the orphans who need help. Most parents are doing their very best to try to send their children to school, but without employment, they have also lost hope and don't know how to make that happen.

We don't know what God has in store for some of these African girls, but I believe they should at least have the chance to be educated. It's not that everyone has to get good grades, but just learning to read and write is very important if you want to have any hope of advancement in life.

Short Hair

In Zimbabwe and Kenya and some other African countries, girls tend to keep their hair short. This is because taking care of it can get really expensive even though some people can do their own hair. In some schools they just require all students to have their hair cut short so that it becomes uniform. It is also done this way so as not to make the ones who can't afford the expense of longer hair feel left out. It's also the same thing with school uniforms. Pretty much all schools use uniforms - private and government schools alike.

Jobs in Rural Areas

The unemployment rate in rural Zimbabwe is over 80% and not everyone who has formal employment gets compensated accordingly. Most people do survive on subsistence farming but the problem comes when there is a drought. Without enough water, the people cannot have food. Some keep cows, goats, sheep and chickens for meat and as a source of wealth, but when there is a drought, the animals will not have enough to eat.

The poverty rate is so high and most people have resolved to small businesses like selling basic necessities on the street corner. The sad thing is that many families survive on $1 a day and this is barely enough to purchase a daily meal. They usually grow enough for their families and if they have left-overs, they sell the produce so they can get money to purchase other things. Most people just live a simple life. They have learned to survive on very little.

Cindi

Another custom is that when children are grown, they are expected to take care of their parents. I guess that in many ways we have the same custom - it just isn't expected in the U.S. like it is in Africa.

Beatrice

Culturally the nursing homes in Zimbabwe are mostly occupied by the white families. There are no 401K's, Medicare or Social Security for the elderly. The locals believe in "Ubuntu", which loosely translates to "I am because of you". Because of this, your children become your retirement plan per say and it's shameful and a disgrace for a black Zimbabwean to neglect their parents or to place them in a nursing home. This is just the custom.

So the cycle is to raise your children in the best way possible and then when you are in your twilight years, your children take care of you. This is the norm and there is no "unfairness" as people in other parts of the world would argue. This isn't true of all families though, because some do have savings and others do get good pensions when they retire. These people can absolutely enjoy a retirement in comfort, complete with travel and leisure. But the majority of the people are dependent on their children, especially since the country is in economic turmoil.

But then how can you take care of your parents if you can't take care of yourself? That's why my parents struggled to make sure that we had the best education, not only so we were on our own feet, but so that we could assist them when they were in need. I do so appreciate what they did for us.

Again, even though it's expected, it doesn't mean that all children take up that responsibility. But if they choose to do so, it is such an honor and a privilege to be able to give back.

Cindi

After having a child, the new parents are to give the mother's parents a gift. That was another interesting custom that I didn't quite understand. It was so nice that Bea and John got to go for a visit so Bea's parents could meet all three boys (I don't think they had met any of them).

Beatrice

When a couple has a child, they are supposed to give their parents a gift such as a goat, some groceries, or some African clothing. Since we couldn't afford to do this earlier, we brought our gift when we went to visit. This is normally done when a bride is pregnant. The daughter is supposed to go back to her parents' home when she is about 8 months pregnant. There the mother would prepare her for how to be a mother, especially if it's her first child. The son-in-law then has to buy a goat and other presents to honor the in-laws and leave his wife there until she gives birth.

Currency

In Kenya, the bank will only exchange bills that are 2007 or newer. That's a good thing to know if you plan to visit there. However, Zimbabwe accepts American money. The dates don't matter there.

Last Names

In Western Kenya when a man gets married, his wife and children take a different last name than his. They literally take the husbands middle name or given name and make it their last name. For example, my husband's full name is John Wesonga Ogomo. Culturally, our children and I should have taken his middle name 'Wesonga' as our last name but since we are here in the US we didn't want to complicate things, so we decided to use Ogomo as the family name. Some people aren't very strict about this anymore though. This is especially true in families where there is only one male child. They can just continue to use their father's last name so as to keep their legacy going.

Reflections

Beatrice

After our mission was over, we got to enjoy a safari in Kenya! Who would have thought that one day I would stand right at the Equator between the Northern and Southern hemispheres! At this moment, my geography lessons with my high school teacher, Mr. Mutenzwa, came alive!

I personally know that it might be easy for someone to say that Cindi chose to go on this trip because she just has the money. Well, there are many people out there who have the money but they choose what or who they want to spend it on. Cindi just chose something that not many people would, but I'm forever grateful that she chose to do so. She did not let my dream die just like that. Many have had dreams and they are still waiting for their dreams to come true. Mine didn't even seem like a dream at all because as soon as I was done dreaming, God made it come true.

Some people do get those little whispers but they choose to ignore them. Well I'm glad and thankful that Cindi didn't ignore it, for it changed many people's lives. I didn't even know that I would get changed in the process, but that is what has happened to me from this experience. It's something that I'm still learning, but I now know that life is not about me alone and I should live my life every day in full acknowledgement that how I live each day impacts many others, one way or another - relatives and strangers alike.

I asked Cindi how she managed to do all this without even putting much thought to it. She said she doesn't look at it in terms of money. That's a lesson learned right there. She said that God has blessed her so that she can bless others and that's what she is doing. I know God had us meet for such a reason and I will grab what I have learned from her and run with the torch, showing others what it means to love without boundaries. I am also very grateful that I set my pride aside and started cleaning - something I thought I would never do, but I did. And for that I know God was trying to show me that it wasn't about me, but to Him be the glory.

Law of Life

When a newspaper reporter interviewed a farmer who grew award-winning corn each year he entered his corn in the state fair, it was revealed that the farmer shared his seed corn with his neighbors. Perplexed, the reporter asked, "How can you afford to share your best seed corn with your neighbors when they are entering their corn in competition with yours each year?" The farmer smiled knowingly and explained, "The wind picks up pollen from the ripening corn and swirls it from field to field. If my neighbors grow inferior corn, cross-pollination will steadily degrade the quality of my corn. If I am to grow good corn, I must help my neighbors grow good corn." So it is with our lives. Those who want to live meaningfully and well must help enrich the lives of others. *For the value of a life is measured by the lives it touches.* And those who choose to be happy must help others find happiness, for the welfare of each is bound up with the welfare of all. Call it power of collectivity. Call it a principle of success. Call it a law of life. The fact remains, *"None of us truly wins, until we all win."* In life, when you help the people around you to be good, you surely become the best. Always bear in mind that "Real happiness is helping others".

—Author Unknown

Beatrice

As I gave much thought to my relationship with Cindi, I thought surely she is like the farmer who shared his good seed. Most of us tend to withhold whatever good things we might have in our lives, not knowing that it is actually more of a blessing to share. Cindi didn't only choose to share with the communities we went to visit. She started with me - sharing a smile, a hug, a listening ear, her time and her generosity. I wonder what would have happened if she chose not to share any one of these things. What I like most about this whole thing is that many will come to know Christ through the books that she has written and also through the acts of kindness we were able to carry out while in Africa. Of course, most people would want to know why someone would be concerned about them to the point of just giving their time and money. I don't know about you, but I would want to know. Out of that curiosity, many will come to know Christ.

No one can do anything in life on their own, though there are a few people who might say they did it completely by themselves. What they may not realize is that God gave them life and the ability to succeed. I look at it this way; Cindi planted a good seed in me and I ought not to keep the seed to myself after harvest. I do not want this good seed to go to waste, so I will take it upon myself to make sure that I share the good seed with others so I don't lose it. What a powerful lesson I have learned.

We also encouraged the church community in Muziti, Rusape to practice sharing the good seed. We purchased more than 300 bags of cornmeal and challenged them to share with the other members of the community, regardless of the fact that they themselves needed more than 1 bag per family. Because of the drought, cornmeal is their staple food. They pretty much use it daily for preparing meals. In such a situation like that God will surely not leave His children hungry, because sharing is never a bad thing. With that I am learning daily to think less of myself and bless others who might be in more need than I am.

Grace's Garden - Beatrice

When God told us to plant a garden we didn't even know what impact it was going to have on the community. The local elementary school asked Grace if they could bring some of the students to her home to learn more about gardening. So now this garden has become a blessing to the community in more ways than we anticipated, and we continue hoping and trusting God that a lot more good will come out of it.

Cindi

I'm sure God is smiling down on Grace because He has blessed her with the best looking garden in the whole community! Now she will be 'sharing her seed' by instructing the children how to tend a garden so they can help their parents survive.

I have to laugh because her chickens are multiplying like crazy!! She almost has too many to count! God is truly showing His favor to Grace because of her obedience and for her heart for others in the community.

Cindi - My Dream and How This Experience Changed Me

I believe that for a very long time I have wanted to make a difference in people's lives, starting with their material needs and then hopefully pointing them to Jesus, the One who is passionate about them. I have done what I could from the comfort of my home town, never wanting to travel far away to see in person what life was like for others around the world.

But now that I have gone and experienced a little bit of the other side, it's hard to go back to "life as usual". I want this to change me for a lifetime - not just for a week or a month. I think about my new friends almost daily. God has definitely put a burden on my heart for them, and for that, I am very grateful. I don't want to live my life just to please me. My heart is to see the needs of people around me everywhere I go – whether at the store, at work or around the world.

God is showing me that I *can* make a difference! And even though I usually can't see the results of what is happening in people's hearts, I know that I can at least cause them to think about their lives and their destiny. I pray I will see many of them in heaven one day. I can't think of any better purpose to live my life for. I desire joy in my life and I have found that giving brings me more joy than anything else I can think of!

Beatrice – My Overall Experience Throughout Our Visit to Both Countries

As I sat down and pondered all the preparations to go to Kenya and Zimbabwe and what we had managed to do and plan in a span of less than 5 months, I could not stop thinking of how amazing God is. He made sure that everything that needed to be done was provided for. Some people had prayed for our trip, some had donated towards the trip (*See below*), while others were there for support. We couldn't have asked for any more.

One thing I know about myself is that I can be selfish. Let's face it. Most of us are, but not always in a bad way. Whenever we get something or an opportunity opens up, we usually think of ourselves first. Then if we already have that thing or if it doesn't benefit us, we may think of those in our circle of life - most often our friends and family.

As I have mentioned before, I have definitely received help from various people on different occasions, but this adventure was different. Even as I sat down to think of it, I knew I had so many relatives, friends or even myself who needed help in so many different ways. I had to battle with it a little bit until I came to a point where God ministered to my heart. I really thought it was going to be easy but as everything started to unfold, when we actually knew that we were to go to Africa, I started having second thoughts. I knew for sure that these thoughts weren't from God.

I am so glad God made sure that I followed through with my dream by sending Cindi my way. I strongly believe that I could have easily fallen into the trap of saying that I have a dream, knowing that it would never come to pass considering the circumstances. My experience in Kenya and Zimbabwe taught me a lot. I could never possibly express it all in words, but all I can say is that it was worth the trip.

Even though I had grown up in Zimbabwe and lived there for many years, I didn't realize how much staying in the US for 13 years had changed me. It was almost as if I saw things with a different set of eyes. When I came to the US, I knew that I wanted to be of help, but mostly to my relatives. I never thought that I had it in me to actually advocate for other people I wasn't even related to. Even when everything seems not to make sense, God always has a way of turning it around. Most of what we did during our trip didn't quite make sense to many people, but God knew exactly what He was doing in my life.

The smiles on many of the children's faces in Kenya were priceless. With most of them you could almost see a smile about to come out, but they were in awe and disbelief. They probably thought that they were dreaming so you couldn't really see their smile. But the satisfaction I got is what I wouldn't trade for anything. It's just one of those things that one can't really explain in words but once you experience it, you will know exactly what I am talking about. In other words, just being Gods' messenger is such an awesome task, and you could never go wrong by following when He asks you to go. I was even shocked at the boldness I had. I knew for sure that it wasn't me. It had to be God because I am not like that on any normal day.

As we gave out the shoes to the kids, my heart was filled with so much pain. It was so hard to look at some of the children's feet that were cracked and filled with dust. Just trying to understand why certain people had to suffer so much is something that I still can't wrap my head around. Only God knows, and as much as I try to question why, I know I won't get an answer – at least not in this life.

My spirit was troubled. Even though I showed a smile on my face, a lot was going through my head. I know God is there but I'm sure there are many people who struggle with the thought that maybe He isn't there – at least not for them. I had to fight the thoughts in my mind because of the bad thoughts that kept coming up.

Cindi

For those who contributed towards our trip, I am pleased to say that everything you gave was used for projects we did while in Africa. None of the money was used for our travel expenses. That means that you had a huge part in all that we did and for that, we say a big "Thank You!!"

Ongoing Projects

As Beatrice was sending out Facebook posts along the way on our journey, she was getting questions about our 'organization' and who we were. People were also wondering if we could help their villages or their loved ones. It was heartbreaking to realize that what we did was just the tip of the iceberg.

Bea's niece, Zenani, was one who was requesting help. She and her family members had been going to a hospital in Africa to pray for the patients there. They realized that the people were very hungry and found out that they only received a bowl of porridge to eat in the morning. That is the only food provided for the day. Otherwise they have to purchase food on their own. But most of the patients are very poor and they don't have the money to buy more food.

Zenani asked if there was any way we could help with funds to get food to the people. After going back and forth with her, we decided to start with twenty people (the hospital staff asked her to focus on the children). They wouldn't let her go directly into the rooms for distribution. Instead they asked the parents to come and get the food for their child. The first time she went, almost 60 mothers showed up for food! I'm thinking God must have multiplied what she brought (like He did with the loaves and the fish) because in her plan she only had enough for twenty children.

Zenani and her family deliver food about twice a week either to the hospital, the prison or the orphanage. They give each person three pieces of fruit (an apple, an orange and a banana). It's not much food considering the amount of people, but she is making a big difference in each person she has reached out to. I am in awe of Zenani and her family for their hearts for the people. They saw a need and they are doing what they can to meet that need. They are faithfully giving of their time to minister to hurting people.

We also sent some books for her to pass out with the food. Some of the books were put in patients' rooms and others were put in the children's learning center. They also want to share the message that there is a Heavenly Father who loves these precious people very much.

Again, can you imagine going to the hospital and not receiving proper meals? The prisons and orphanages don't have enough food either. Sometimes I think we forget just how good we have things in America and how blessed we really are.

We also hope to send some children to school and help them get an education that hopefully will change their lives. Again, it feels like our efforts won't have that much of an impact because there are so many who need help with these costs. Because of that, we know we need to stay focused on what we *can* do and then trust God to do what only *He can do* to make up the difference.

I was told about the 'starfish theory' from a good friend of ours. If you haven't heard it before, this is how it goes:

A little girl was down at the seashore. The tide had washed in millions of starfish and she was picking them up and throwing them back in the water one at a time. A man walked by and asked what she was doing. When she explained that the starfish were dying and she was putting them back in the water, he told her that what she was doing wouldn't make a difference because there were too many. As she picked up the next one she replied, "It made a difference for that one!"

I love that story because it reminds me that even though the needs are so great and I couldn't possibly meet them all, I can make a difference in the lives of the people God has called me to touch. And what is done will make a difference for them and for each one they touch because of the kindness they have received. We each just need to focus on what we have been called to do and leave the 'ripple effect' to God.

How This Trip Changed Me

Beatrice

With the different experiences I've had in life, I know that God is sovereign. You may never know what He has in store for your life if you don't ask Him. You never know where He might send you and you never know your future, but God knows the plans He has for you.

Jeremiah 29:11 says: *"For I know the plans I have for you,"* declares the Lord, *"plans to prosper you and not to harm you, plans to give you hope and a future."*

If most of us knew what the future held, this world would be a completely different place. It is however good not to know about the future because most of us might have run away from what God has intended for us. I might have done the same thing. I am not positive, but it is good to guard our thoughts as our minds do not always think the best.

The devil is very real and he constantly looks for opportunities in our lives where he can come in to steal, kill and destroy our purpose and our dreams. I have lost so many relatives through the years when I was still back in Zimbabwe and after I came to the US. This includes parents, aunts, uncles, cousins, siblings, and grandparents. As each and every one of these people passed on, I kept asking God why and how I was ever going to live life without them. I don't have all the answers but He continues to comfort me even now. And He gives me strength to go on. The more I experience life, the more I realize that I need Him more and more every day.

After all has been said and done, what exactly am I trying to get across? Well it's not rocket science. It's really very simple. An African girl once had a dream of coming to America. She didn't know how she would come. She had her own selfish agenda; to go to school, start working and make money for herself and her family but she never thought much of helping those outside of her family. But God opened up a door for her through Heather. I don't know what I was going to do after I got rich. I actually never thought about it.

Well then, what happened to that African girl? She did get rich, but not in the way she expected. Life happened and along the way, she met Cindi, who had a different perspective of life altogether. Cindi had never been to Africa and never wished to go there. But God gave her a big heart for African people that she didn't even know she had until she met me. Then God put a burden on my heart and He also put the same burden on Cindi's heart. Together we decided to make our dream come true.

But something happened after our trip to Africa. I thought this was a one-time episode and that we were just going to come back and move on with our lives, but apparently not. God still has more for us to do and we are going to be obedient. How could all this have been possible? God had us cross paths for a reason. He wanted to target certain people to hear His Word through our distribution of the books.

I am so glad God planned it this way because I have no idea how I would have been able to share the Word with many, or to bring anyone to Christ if I had tried to do it myself. I know we are to bring others to Christ and I always questioned myself as to how I was going to be able to do that. Well now I have no excuse, for God made sure that I had all the resources I needed.

Many might hear about Christ, but not all of them will come to Him. I know that among the many that will get the opportunity to read the books, some will come to Christ. It might not be right away, but a seed will be planted, and I am grateful to be among those who are spreading the Word of God. I say this because nothing on this earth matters more than to know Christ and to be certain of where you will spend eternity. I actually sit down in amazement and wonder how God chose to use me. I know I may have sung a few songs and even prayed and asked for God to use me, but did I really know what I was asking for? I wonder.

I've always heard people say you need to give back to the community and I've often wondered what that would feel or look like. I have come to know that it doesn't necessarily have to be the community you grew up in, but I can at least make a difference somehow. All this is to thank all of those who have helped me from childhood until now. I have been helped all my life and as God has blessed me, I need to help others with the little I have. And then as He blesses me more, I need to be a good steward of that too. That being said, I know God is using both Cindi and me to help others, to encourage them, and to give them hope for life.

Cindi

I have such mixed feelings when it comes to giving and asking people for money to help with projects. Honestly, I would rather do it by myself than to have to ask others to give. It seems like I always have to remind myself that there are a lot of people who need to experience the joy of giving and if given the opportunity, it just might be the thing that gets them started on their own journey. Of course, there are always those who are constantly looking for opportunities to give and can't wait to join in and be a part of something bigger and I am so grateful for their support and encouragement.

Then there's the fact that I'm being selfish by trying to keep the blessing all to myself by not sharing the needs with others. Sometimes I forget that we will all share in the reward when we work together. It doesn't matter if you are the one giving, praying or supporting in other ways – each part is vital and each person will be rewarded for their part. But how will they know there's a need if no one tells them about it?

In Matthew 6:1, 3-4 it says: *"Take care! Don't do your good deeds publicly, to be admired, for then you will lose the reward from your Father in heaven. But when you do a kindness to someone, do it secretly*

- don't tell your left hand what your right hand is doing. And your Father who knows all secrets will reward you."

I agree with this but I also struggle with it. I don't share my stories with you to boast about what I have done. My hope is to entice you to try new things for yourself. Some of my best ideas have come about because someone shared their giving story with me. We need to encourage each other to be the best we can possibly be – and that definitely includes teaching how to give well. I think there's a fine line between boasting and encouraging.

The Bible also says in Hebrews 10:24: *"Let us consider how to stimulate one another to love and good deeds..."* How do we encourage and stimulate one another if we don't share our "God stories"? I love to share the excitement of others as they relate their giving stories to me! Many times our joy is doubled when we have someone to confide in. There are also times when our giving is best done in secret. I think we'll know the difference.

So much that we see in the world teaches us to pursue riches by grasping and hoarding all the things we acquire along the way. But the way to attain true riches which will last for eternity is to let them go and freely give to those in need. That's how we lay up our treasures in heaven, where they won't rot or be stolen. When we put our treasures in heaven, our hearts follow. We become mindful of others and we do all we can to help with their needs.

That's what the Bible talks about in Matthew 6:19-21. *"Don't store up treasures here on earth where they can erode away or may be stolen. Store them in heaven where they will never lose their value and are safe from thieves. If your profits are in heaven, your heart will be there too."*

I don't know if we ever fully 'arrive' in this pursuit. But the journey of getting there is an exciting one! What if you made it your goal to touch as many lives as possible while you are on this earth? I believe that is part of everyone's purpose. We aren't put here to get all we can and to store it all up for ourselves. That can quickly drain the life right out of us! It's probably a big cause of stress and depression because when we are living for ourselves and for our own purposes and pleasures, life has little meaning.

I find it interesting that in Africa the suicide rate is much lower than it is in America. I can't state facts or statistics regarding this, but it seems to me that many are looking for fulfillment in the wrong places. And when life gets hard, we aren't sure where to turn. I believe the answer is to look past yourself to the needs of those around you. As you begin to invest in the lives of others, you become fulfilled yourself.

You may not have much money but you can offer time or a listening ear. Or you may have a lot of money and not a lot of time. Be creative with whatever you have been given. What you have is less important than what you do with what you have. I had a picture once that said "Your walk talks and your talk talks, but your walk talks more than your talk talks!" What are your actions saying to those around you about what is most important in your life? What are you doing with what God has entrusted to you?

Try many new ways of giving yourself away to others. Maybe you will be one who inspires others to do great things. And who knows, they may take it a step further and inspire you! Don't let jealousy get in the way. No one wins when we spend our time comparing ourselves with others. If we all work together and give what we have, just think of the impact we could make! One person can't do it alone but when they find others to come alongside of them, watch out! Together they just might become world changers!

I think about our dream. It started out with sending shoes to Africa. In the end, we got to take them personally, offer medical treatment and hand out food to hungry people. Over a thousand people were impacted because Beatrice had a dream! But just as importantly, other people believed in our dream and did what they could to help us make it a reality. And then they prayed for us diligently and God multiplied all that we did because of it.

Now we are at a place where we are willing to go back if that is what God has for us. But we don't want to get ahead of God and just make our own plans. In the meantime, we are doing outreaches periodically. We have people we can trust to carry them out in our absence.

Besides the hospital, prison and orphanage outreach, we hope to raise funds to buy food again for the people to distribute (possibly even give them two bags this time – one to keep and one to share), send money so they can do more jigger treatments, and whatever else God may show us.

One of the recent challenges we have run into since getting back is that it's harder to send money for projects. The people in Zimbabwe are only able to take anywhere from $20.00 to $100.00 out of the bank at a time because the country is short on money. Beatrice has had to get creative in finding ways to do this. The people who do have jobs there are required to put their paychecks in the bank but they can only take the money out in small increments.

Most of the wells in the area where we visited have dried up because the people couldn't afford to dig them deep enough. We are praying that God brings rain in the months following the planting season so the wells will supply the water needed and the crops will grow and produce an abundant harvest.

One of the reasons we decided to write this book is to raise awareness and funds so we can do more projects. God may not always send us to Africa but we want to be ready and obedient whenever and wherever He wants to take us.

Life can easily become like a checklist when you aren't listening to God, but it can be such an adventure when you live with your eyes wide open to the possibilities all around you! When I wrote the YOLT book, I said: *"When many people think of what God has for them, they think that it must be something unexciting and probably involves being a missionary in Africa or some remote place for the rest of their lives. God has a special purpose for each one of us right where we are. And I guarantee that if you are one who is chosen to go to Africa, it will be the most exciting adventure of your life!"* God must have been smiling when I wrote that, knowing that He was getting ready to take me there!

If you feel your life lacks purpose, ask God to give you a dream and then show you how to make it become a reality. He loves to answer those prayers! You were designed *on purpose for a purpose.*

God wants to use ordinary people to do extraordinary things. It's not about being qualified, just available. When I look at my ordinary life – a high school graduate with no college degree, a wife, mother and grandmother – I have asked myself many times, "Why would God choose *me?*" I have no special skills. What an honor to be chosen by Almighty God to partner with Him in His work on this earth! It doesn't get any better than that!

God has purposes for each one of us and He calls us to join forces with Him and with others. We have to choose whether we will listen to Him or follow our own dreams.

"He who shuts his ears to the cries of the poor will be ignored in his own time of need." Proverbs 21:13

Maybe all of this sounds foreign to you because you don't know the Lord personally. You may have thought that the stories in the Bible are made up and not reality. But they are true, and God still does miracles today through ordinary people like you and me.

I challenge you to go through each day looking for God and the many ways He is providing for you and blessing you all day long. Maybe it's as basic as the fact that He gives life and breath to you. There is no such thing as a 'coincidence'. Those are just the times when God chooses to remain anonymous. He has the whole world in His hands and He cares about *every* detail of your life.

The joy God gives is unlike anything this world has to offer. His joy doesn't depend on what we have or who we know. It's about knowing Him and fulfilling His purposes for us. That's how we find joy that's overflowing! And the best part about it is that the rewards God gives last for *eternity*!! He doesn't give out trophies that rust or break. I don't know what the rewards will be, but I do know they are worth pursuing with my whole heart!

I challenge you to consider your life and what you are living for. If this book has sparked any dreams in your life, I would love to hear about them and how God helps you in the process! Let's keep encouraging others to do and to give our very best in this journey of life. Wouldn't it be amazing to see what could happen if we all experienced the power of our dreams! Our lives and the lives of others would never be the same! Will you join us in our attempt to change the world for the better?

All proceeds from this and any of the other books listed will go for projects in Africa or other places we are called to go. Thank you for supporting us in our efforts and for sharing the reward with us! And thanks for partnering in our dreams!

Other books include:

YOLT
(You Only Live Twice)

YOLT JR.
(younger readers)

CHOICES
(young adults and older)

JESUS LOVES ME, THIS I KNOW!
(infants and young children – 2017 release)

You can find these books at
www.YoltPublishing.com

If this book has encouraged you in your dreams, please share your story at cj.yolt@gmail.com or on our Facebook page.

If you would like to see a short video of our trip to Africa, visit our website or Facebook.com/yoltcompassion

www.ingramcontent.com/pod-product-compliance
Lightning Source LLC
Chambersburg PA
CBHW071459070426
42452CB00041B/1932